Kantar on Kontract

Eddie Kantar

MASTER POINT PRESS | TORONTO, ONTARIO

Master Point Press
331 Douglas Ave.
Toronto, Ontario, Canada
M5M 1H2
(416) 781-0351
Website: http://www.masterpointpress.com
Email: info@masterpointpress.com

National Library of Canada Cataloguing in Publication

Kantar, Edwin B., 1932-
        Kantar on kontract / Eddie Kantar.

ISBN 1-894154-68-1

        1. Contract bridge. I. Title. II. Title: Kantar on kontract.

GV1282.3.K36 2004   795.41'5   C2003-906626-6

Editor   Ray Lee
Cover and interior design   Olena S. Sullivan/New Mediatrix
Interior format and copy editing   Luise Lee

Printed in Canada by Webcom Ltd.

1 2 3 4 5 6 7   09 08 07 06 05 04

Contents

Contents

Introduction

I have been writing bridge columns since my university days, and even back then I was ghosting syndicated columns, too (you don't want to know what they paid me). Then, finally, in the early sixties I got my own column in the *Valley Green Sheet*, a San Fernando Valley paper with a large circulation. Eventually though, after some years, the paper bought into a syndicate which supplied them with a bridge column, so out I went. Then I landed a column in the *Evening Outlook*, a now defunct Santa Monica newspaper. All this time I was still feeding material to several syndicated columnists who always seemed to be in need of another 'good hand'. The bottom line is that I saved all these columns over the years (never throw away a good bridge hand, there's always someone out there who hasn't seen it).

So the process of 'writing' this book was to read through all this material, toss out the losers and keep the winners. I wound up with about two hundred real winners; don't ask how many real losers I pitched. Then my publisher helped to refine the list even further, to the *crème de la crème* that you will find in these pages. There's been some discreet editing, too, of course: we all had a good laugh over the column that originally described Benito Garozzo as a 'promising new young player'.

In making the final selection, I hoped to combine equal amounts of humor and instruction, along with some great stories and great bridge hands. But most of all, I wanted it to be something people would enjoy reading. So — enjoy!

Eddie Kantar

Bridge players like to set records. Well, here's one Paul Soloway and I set that we would both like to forget.

The Hall of Shame

Neither vul.

North
♠ A K Q 6
♡ K
◇ A Q 10 4
♣ K 7 6 4

West (Soloway)
♠ J 5 4
♡ 6 5
◇ K J 9 3 2
♣ Q J 5

East (me)
♠ 10 9 8 2
♡ A 10 9 3 2
◇ 8
♣ A 9 8

South
♠ 7 3
♡ Q J 8 7 4
◇ 7 6 5
♣ 10 3 2

West	North	East	South
	2◇	pass	2♡
pass	2♠	pass	3♣
pass	4♣	all pass	

Opening lead: ♣5

Are you impressed with the contract? Perhaps an explanation is in order.

North-South were playing a Roman 2◇ opening which showed a powerful three-suited hand with 17-24 HCP, the short suit unknown. South bid 2♡, telling North that if hearts was one of his suits, 2♡ would be a wonderful contract. North's bid of 2♠ showed heart shortness. South decided that it would be better to play in clubs rather than spades and bid 3♣; North didn't get the joke and raised. So now you know.

The best lead against one of these auctions is usually a trump so Paul decided to lead the five from the ♣Q-J-5.

Kantar on Kontract

1

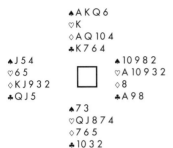

```
              ♠ A K Q 6
              ♡ K
              ◇ A Q 10 4
              ♣ K 7 6 4
♠ J 5 4                      ♠ 10 9 8 2
♡ 6 5                        ♡ A 10 9 3 2
◇ K J 9 3 2                  ◇ 8
♣ Q J 5                      ♣ A 9 8
              ♠ 7 3
              ♡ Q J 8 7 4
              ◇ 7 6 5
              ♣ 10 3 2
```

Dummy played low and I cleverly inserted the ♣8 which lost to the ten. At Trick 2 declarer led a heart to the king and ace. Never dreaming that Paul had underled the queen-jack of clubs, and under the delusion that South had four of them, I exited with the ace and a club.

And so it came to pass that Paul and I, with a combined defensive trump holding of the AQJ985, took one trick! Surely this record will stand forever. Oh yes, we still managed to beat the bloody hand one trick. Two people who had never played bridge before in their lives would have beaten it two or three tricks.

Can you do worse?

How many times has your partner started with ten tricks and ended with less? How does starting with twelve and ending with eight grab you? It's called a multiple compression play.

N-S vul.

North
- ♠ J 10 4
- ♡ 6 3
- ◇ 8 6 2
- ♣ A 10 9 8 7

West
- ♠ 7 6 3
- ♡ K Q 9 7 4
- ◇ 10 5
- ♣ 6 5 3

East
- ♠ K 8
- ♡ A 10 8 2
- ◇ A Q 9 7 3
- ♣ J 4

South
- ♠ A Q 9 5 2
- ♡ J 5
- ◇ K J 4
- ♣ K Q 2

West	North	East	South
		1◇	1♠
pass	2♠	pass	4♠
dbl!	all pass		

Opening lead: ◇10

South, Harvey Cohen, Los Angeles bridge expert and stock-broker (in that order — until this hand) was faced with playing 4♠, doubled by West.

'What could West possibly have for his double?' mused Cohen as East rose with the ◇A at Trick 1 and returned the ◇9 to Harvey's jack. Certainly he must have the ♠K and a high heart honor, but what else? Well, if West has three spades headed by the king, the hand is hopeless. West will win a spade finesse and lead a heart over to East to get a diamond ruff.

Cohen hatched a plan. He would try to sneak a spade by West. Cohen led a low spade towards dummy. If West has the king and ducks, dummy's jack wins, a spade can be led to the ace and clubs started. If West has at least three clubs, one heart can be discarded before West can ruff in with the ♠K. It was a wonderful plan...

A low spade was led and when East won the king, Cohen turned purple. East returned a diamond, West ruffed and two hearts later Cohen was down 500. As the cards lie, declarer can actually take twelve tricks! Say Cohen enters dummy with the ♣A at Trick 3 and takes a winning spade finesse by leading the jack. A low spade is led to the ace and when the king appears, Cohen wins the ace, cashes the king and queen of clubs and enters dummy with the ♠10, chucking both of his hearts on winning clubs.

Harvey swears that his advice on stocks and bonds does not match his play of this hand.

Smile...

Candid Camera should have been on hand to catch the expression on West's face after he made his opening lead on this hand from a National Championship pair game in Cleveland.

Both vul.

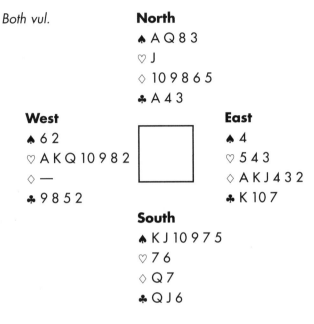

North
♠ A Q 8 3
♡ J
◊ 10 9 8 6 5
♣ A 4 3

West
♠ 6 2
♡ A K Q 10 9 8 2
◊ —
♣ 9 8 5 2

East
♠ 4
♡ 5 4 3
◊ A K J 4 3 2
♣ K 10 7

South
♠ K J 10 9 7 5
♡ 7 6
◊ Q 7
♣ Q J 6

West	North	East	South
			2♠[1]
3♡	4♠	5♡	pass
pass	5♠	all pass	

1. Weak

Opening lead: ♡9

Anxious to get a diamond ruff, West led the nine of hearts! Not all that unreasonable given that East had supported the suit. When West let out a muffled scream upon seeing the dummy, the whole world knew what had happened. Declarer made the most of his good fortune. He crossed to his hand with a trump, ruffed a heart, cashed a second high trump and led a diamond from dummy. East could take his A-K, but there was nothing he could do to prevent South from establishing two diamonds to discard two clubs. Five spades bid and made. Another imaginative lead down the tubes.

The irony of the hand is that if West is a bit less imaginative the hand can be defeated two tricks. All West has to do is lead a high heart and shift to a club. Actually the blame for this debacle rests with East. East should double 5♠, holding the A-K of diamonds plus the king of clubs facing a partner who has made a three-level overcall. Please.

If East had doubled, West would not have felt compelled to make a newspaper column lead. Also, there would have been no story.

Many players have no trouble at all deciding whether to over-ruff declarer or dummy if they can. They just do it. Those players had better take a look at this deal.

To ruff or not to ruff

Neither vul.

North
♠ Q 2
♡ 8 6
◇ K Q 9 5
♣ J 10 9 7 6

West
♠ A 8
♡ Q 3 2
◇ J 4 3 2
♣ A K 5 4

East
♠ K 9 3
♡ 9 7
◇ A 10 7 6
♣ Q 8 3 2

South
♠ J 10 7 6 5 4
♡ A K J 10 5 4
◇ 8
♣ —

West	North	East	South
1♣	pass	1◇	1♠
1NT	pass	pass	4♡
pass	4♠	dbl	all pass

Opening lead: ♣A (ace from ace-king)

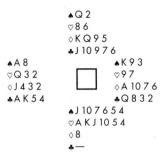

```
            ♠Q 2
            ♡8 6
            ◇K Q 9 5
            ♣J 10 9 7 6
♠A 8                      ♠K 9 3
♡Q 3 2          ☐        ♡9 7
◇J 4 3 2                 ◇A 10 7 6
♣A K 5 4                 ♣Q 8 3 2
            ♠J 10 7 6 5 4
            ♡A K J 10 5 4
            ◇8
            ♣—
```

South ruffed the opening lead and correctly attacked his side suit, hearts, playing the ace-king and ruffing a heart with the ♠Q. East overtrumped with the king. End of defense. With the remaining spades divided 2-2, South wound up losing two spades and a diamond.

Now let's see what happens if East doesn't overruff. Declarer leads a spade from dummy to the jack and ace. East gets two more spade tricks with the K-9, another trick with the ◇A, and the hand is defeated one trick.

What's the rule? There isn't really a rule, but it is generally wrong to overtrump an honor when you will make a trick with your honor regardless, especially if you also hold an intermediate spot card that might promote to a further winner.

Consider this position, where spades are trumps and West has a chance to overtrump declarer... and shouldn't:

North

♠ 2

West (you)

♠ Q 9 4 3

East

♠ 5

South

♠ A K J 10 8 7 6

Pretend that East leads a suit that neither declarer, South, nor you have, and South trumps with the jack. If you overtrump with the queen, that will be your last trump trick. However, if you discard, the Q9xx are suddenly worth two trump tricks. Amen.

When almost every player in a championship event makes the same defensive error on the same hand, you begin to realize the game cannot be played mechanically. There is still a premium for clear thinking.

Sorry, got to think

N-S vul.

North
♠ J 9 7 3
♡ 9 8 5 4
◇ A J
♣ Q 9 3

West
♠ 4 2
♡ A K 2
◇ Q 4 3 2
♣ K J 4 2

East
♠ —
♡ Q 10
◇ 10 9 8 7 6
♣ A 10 8 7 6 5

South
♠ A K Q 10 8 6 5
♡ J 7 6 3
◇ K 5
♣ —

West	North	East	South
	pass	pass	4♠
pass	pass	4NT[1]	pass
5♣	5♠	pass	pass
dbl	all pass		

1. Two-suited takeout including diamonds.

Opening lead: ♡K

When this hand was played in the Blue Ribbon Pairs, many South players bought the hand for four or five spades and invariably made five even though there are three inescapable heart losers. What happened?

What happened was that every West player who saw partner play the ♡ 10 at trick one couldn't wait to cash the ace and maybe give partner a ruff. What partner was

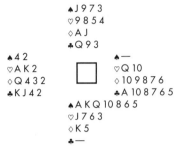

          ♠ J 9 7 3
          ♡ 9 8 5 4
          ◇ A J
          ♣ Q 9 3
♠ 4 2   ♠ —
♡ A K 2   ♡ Q 10
◇ Q 4 3 2   ◇ 10 9 8 7 6
♣ K J 4 2   ♣ A 10 8 7 6 5
          ♠ A K Q 10 8 6 5
          ♡ J 7 6 3
          ◇ K 5
          ♣ —

supposed to ruff with remains a mystery. Surely South has seven spades for his vulnerable pre-empt, which leaves East with a void. The truth is that if West leads any card other than the ace of hearts at Trick 2, the hand can be defeated as South cannot avoid three heart losers.

There is a lesson here. Think before you play and if the bidding tells you that partner is void in trumps, it's not a Phi Beta Kappa play to try to give partner a ruff. Yes, partner might have had the Q10x of hearts, but where are declarer's heart losers going?

Not so fast

More contracts are lost at trick one than at any other trick. Not this one.

Neither vul.

North
♠ K 4
♡ A Q 7 3
◇ A K Q 5 4 3
♣ 2

West
♠ Q J 8 7 6 3
♡ K 2
◇ J 10 7
♣ J 10

East
♠ A 5
♡ 9 8 4
◇ 9 8 2
♣ A Q 9 8 3

South
♠ 10 9 2
♡ J 10 6 5
◇ 6
♣ K 7 6 5 4

West	North	East	South
			pass
2♠[1]	dbl	pass	3♡
pass	4♡	all pass	

1. Weak

Opening lead: ♠Q

East should have raised to 3♠ preemptively, which might have made it more difficult for North-South to reach 4♡ — not that 4♡ is all that great a contract with the ♠A lurking over the king.

Given South's spade spots, the temptation to cover the queen at Trick 1 is pretty strong. But if South reviews the bidding, South will realize that East has A-x of spades and if the ♠K is played, East can win and return a spade, and a third spade is an uncomfortable (read: impossible) play for South to handle. (Ruffing with the ♡Q results in losing a later trump trick.) South ducked the ♠Q, East won the spade continuation, cashed the ♣A and exited a high diamond.

This was a thinking defense. If South and West each had two diamonds, South would not be able to get back to his hand to take the heart finesse as West would be able to overruff South on the third round. Alas, South had a single-ton diamond and was able to ruff a diamond, take the heart finesse and claim when both red suits came rolling in...

The deal has an amusing epilogue. The hand is from an Intercity match between the Twin Cities and Los Angeles won by Los Angeles. On the diagrammed deal, the L.A team bid and made 4♡ when declarer correctly ducked the open-ing lead. When Knute Dockman was North for the Twin Cities, he bid 3♣ over the opening 2♠ bid — he and his partner, Dave Clarren, were using this call as a takeout dou-ble over Weak Twos. Clarren responded 3♡ and just as Knute was about to raise to game, East started rearranging his cards and flashed the ace of spades!

Dockman now feared a spade lead through his king in a contract of 4♡ so he bid 3NT! East led a club and Dockman began to wonder if maybe he hadn't seen the ace of clubs and not the ace of spades! Fearlessly he played the king from dummy, took the heart finesse, ran the hearts, ran the diamonds and wound up making five notrump which rep-resented a small gain for the Twin Cities.

Knute swears he is going to be more careful next time. If someone flashes an ace, he is going to take a better look.

In Toronto there lives a bridge player named Cass. He's a good player and he's an action player. Whenever he's in a game he stirs up trouble — for one side or the other. Here's an example of Cass in action playing money bridge.

Both vul.

North
♠ K 10 2
♡ A K J 10
♢ 2
♣ A J 9 4 3

West
♠ Q J 9 8 7
♡ Q 3 2
♢ 10 5
♣ 8 6 2

East
♠ A 6 5 4 3
♡ 9 8 7 6
♢ K 4 3
♣ 10

South
♠ —
♡ 5 4
♢ A Q J 9 8 7 6
♣ K Q 7 5

West	North	East	South
			(Cass)
	1♣	pass	1♡!
pass	2♢!	pass	4NT
pass	5♡	pass	7♢
pass	7♡	all pass	

Opening lead: ♠Q

Talk about being hoist with your own petard. Cass responded 1♡ intending to play a high-level contract in diamonds without getting a heart lead. North tried a reverse on a singleton knowing that he could always support hearts later. When Cass came out of the bushes and bid 7♢, North was ready to take Cass back to his first suit(?). From such sequences come great stories.

Cass ruffed the opening lead in his hand, playing low from dummy, and needed miracles. Many miracles. The first miracle was to hope West had precisely Q-x-x of hearts. A heart was led to the ten and the ace-king brought down the queen and then came the ♡J, drawing East's last trump. First miracle answered. The hand was now being played in notrump.

Next, Cass cashed five clubs. On the fifth club this is what it looked like:

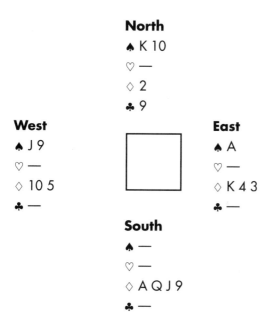

North
♠ K 10
♡ —
◇ 2
♣ 9

West
♠ J 9
♡ —
◇ 10 5
♣ —

East
♠ A
♡ —
◇ K 4 3
♣ —

South
♠ —
♡ —
◇ A Q J 9
♣ —

East had to make a discard. A diamond was instant death as Cass could finesse the diamond and run the suit. Pitching the ♠A simply delayed the agony.

Cass discarded a diamond, cashed the ♠K discarding another diamond, and took the diamond finesse.

Only a diamond lead, East playing low at Trick 1, breaks up the squeeze and defeats the grand. Once again good, solid bidding has paid off.

The third opponent

Who is it that thwarts most great bids made at the bridge table? Partner, of course, who else? Can you imagine the feelings and thoughts that passed through George Zahler's mind when his unnamed partner (if the name Don Krauss comes to mind, never let it be said that you read it here) did the following to him at the Savoy Club one time!

E-W vul.

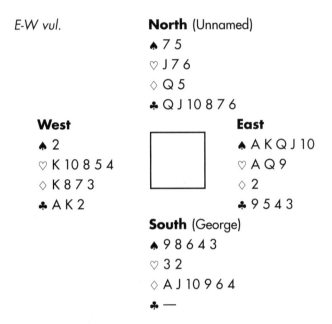

North (Unnamed)
- ♠ 7 5
- ♡ J 7 6
- ◇ Q 5
- ♣ Q J 10 8 7 6

West
- ♠ 2
- ♡ K 10 8 5 4
- ◇ K 8 7 3
- ♣ A K 2

East
- ♠ A K Q J 10
- ♡ A Q 9
- ◇ 2
- ♣ 9 5 4 3

South (George)
- ♠ 9 8 6 4 3
- ♡ 3 2
- ◇ A J 10 9 6 4
- ♣ —

West opened the bidding 1♡ and East jumped to 4NT. At this point George decided to make a 'lead-directing' 5♣ bid! If he had only known that this bid was not going to fall upon deaf ears. West responded 5◇ to show one ace and North, reading the position perfectly, decided to take his 'first' sacrifice in 6♣. East bid six hearts which rolled around to North. Can you see it coming?

All North had to do was pass and lead a club which George would ruff, and his ◇A would be the setting trick. George would be the hero. He would show me the deal and I would write it up. Not so fast. North now made a bid that he was to regret for a long, long, time (even longer after he had seen this write-up). He sacrificed in 7♣. When this was doubled, Zahler was forced to bid 7◊ which both opponents doubled at the same time. George managed to take five trump tricks for down eight! Do not ask about the postmortem; just don't.

What's the best hand you ever held in your life? Bet it's not as good as the South hand here.

Be it never so humble

Both vul.

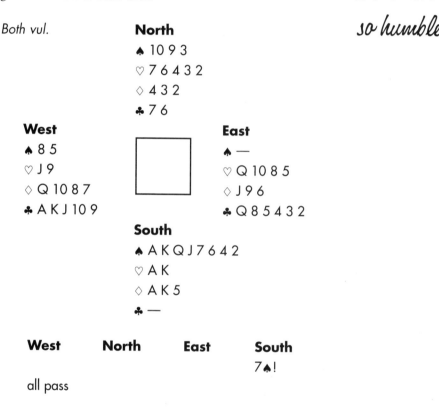

North
- ♠ 10 9 3
- ♡ 7 6 4 3 2
- ◊ 4 3 2
- ♣ 7 6

West
- ♠ 8 5
- ♡ J 9
- ◊ Q 10 8 7
- ♣ A K J 10 9

East
- ♠ —
- ♡ Q 10 8 5
- ◊ J 9 6
- ♣ Q 8 5 4 3 2

South
- ♠ A K Q J 7 6 4 2
- ♡ A K
- ◊ A K 5
- ♣ —

West	North	East	South
			7♠!

all pass

Opening lead: ♣A

Did you notice that East-West have a good save in eight clubs? Too bad those bids were outlawed a long time ago. Of course a sacrifice is only a good move if the opponents can make their contract. If you were in a grand slam in spades with a high club lead, how would you play?

If you didn't notice that the best card in your hand was

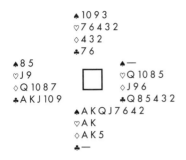

♠ 10 9 3
♡ 7 6 4 3 2
◇ 4 3 2
♣ 7 6

♠ 8 5
♡ J 9
◇ Q 10 8 7
♣ A K J 10 9

♠ —
♡ Q 10 8 5
◇ J 9 6
♣ Q 8 5 4 3 2

♠ A K Q J 7 6 4 2
♡ A K
◇ A K 5
♣ —

the ♠2 and you used it at Trick 1, the hand is over. You can no longer make the grand. In order to make this hand, you have to set up hearts. If hearts are a normal 4-2, you need three dummy entries to set up the suit. The third entry requires you to lead the deuce of spades to dummy's three to get to the established fifth heart. There are actually three traps to avoid:

(1) Not looking over the whole hand before playing to the first trick.

(2) Ruffing the opening lead with the ♠2, your most precious card.

(3) Playing even one round of spades before cashing the ♡AK. You need three spade entries to dummy after the ace-king of hearts have been cashed.

Why you lose at bridge

How do you feel about doubling a slam contract with two aces?

N-S vul.

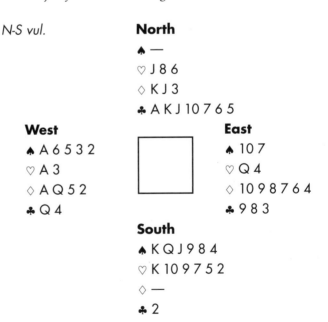

North
♠ —
♡ J 8 6
◇ K J 3
♣ A K J 10 7 6 5

West
♠ A 6 5 3 2
♡ A 3
◇ A Q 5 2
♣ Q 4

East
♠ 10 7
♡ Q 4
◇ 10 9 8 7 6 4
♣ 9 8 3

South
♠ K Q J 9 8 4
♡ K 10 9 7 5 2
◇ —
♣ 2

West	North	East	South
1♠	3♣¹	pass	3♡
pass	4♡	pass	6♡
dbl	all pass		

1. Intermediate

Opening lead: ♠A

S. J. Simon posed the above question in his classic book *Why You Lose at Bridge*. He went on to say that if you answered 'yes', you had better read his book. If you answered 'no', you probably didn't have to. He went on to explain the mathematics of the situation showing how you stood to lose far more than you stood to gain because of the possibility that one of your aces wasn't cashing, not to mention a possible redouble.

Well, if it's not such a good idea to double two good players who get to slam when you have two aces, how does doubling with three aces grab you? Most West players on this deal from a National Championship pairs game could not resist the impulse to double six hearts with three aces; some doubled *four* hearts!

It really doesn't matter which ace is led, but at most tables the first ace to bite the dust was a spade. At Trick 2 the jack of hearts was covered by the queen, king and ace. Panic stricken, West tried to cash the ◊A. No luck there either. South ruffed and had the rest of the tricks as the spades were all good and the club queen came down for good measure.

So the new question is: Would you double a small slam holding all four aces?

Now you see them, now you don't

Bridge is a strange game. Sometimes in a trump contract you count four sure losers, but you wind up with ten tricks anyway. How about counting five losers and still winding up with ten tricks? Maybe the answer is to count tricks instead of losers? It definitely is when you plan to do some trumping in one hand or the other, not to mention crossruffing.

Neither vul.

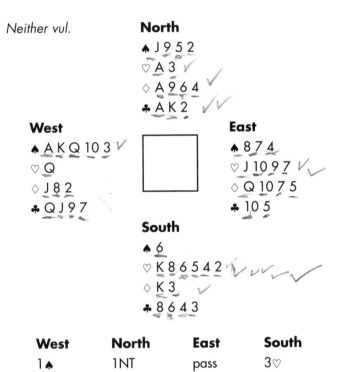

North
♠ J 9 5 2
♡ A 3
♢ A 9 6 4
♣ A K 2

West
♠ A K Q 10 3
♡ Q
♢ J 8 2
♣ Q J 9 7

East
♠ 8 7 4
♡ J 10 9 7
♢ Q 10 7 5
♣ 10 5

South
♠ 6
♡ K 8 6 5 4 2
♢ K 3
♣ 8 6 4 3

West	North	East	South
1♠	1NT	pass	3♡
pass	4♡	all pass	

Opening lead: ♠Q (Q from AKQ — try it, you may like it)

At Trick 2 West shifted to the ♣Q. Declarer won in dummy and followed with a spade ruff in the closed hand. South continued with the king-ace of hearts and got the bad news. He suddenly had two trump losers to go along with the spade he had already lost not to mention two more 'possible' club losers. In fact, with the clubs breaking 4-2, he had two club losers; counting losers you wind up with a depressing five. Now let's count tricks!

Kantar on Kontract

You start with the A-K of hearts, diamonds and clubs for six big ones. If you can trump four times in the closed hand you will have ten! You have already trumped one spade and with the lead in dummy, you trump another. That's two ruffs in the closed hand. Say you continue with the king-ace and a diamond ruff, the third ruff in the closed hand, cross to the ♣A and trump another diamond. Don't look now, but you have ruffed four times in the closed hand and you have ten tricks in spite of having five losers!

And what happened to those five losers? They are still there, but they 'crash'. East still has two high hearts and West has two high clubs but each hand only has two cards left. Two cards can only take two tricks. Count your tricks!

How about those deals where the only way to avoid a ruff is not to draw trumps?

Hands off !

N-S vul.

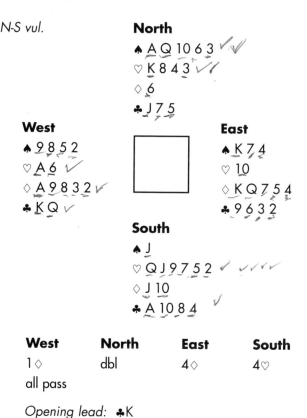

North
- ♠ A Q 10 6 3
- ♡ K 8 4 3
- ◊ 6
- ♣ J 7 5

West
- ♠ 9 8 5 2
- ♡ A 6
- ◊ A 9 8 3 2
- ♣ K Q

East
- ♠ K 7 4
- ♡ 10
- ◊ K Q 7 5 4
- ♣ 9 6 3 2

South
- ♠ J
- ♡ Q J 9 7 5 2
- ◊ J 10
- ♣ A 10 8 4

West	North	East	South
1◊	dbl	4◊	4♡
all pass			

Opening lead: ♣K

```
          ♠ A Q 10 6 3
          ♡ K 8 4 3
          ◇ 6
          ♣ J 7 5
♠ 9 8 5 2              ♠ K 7 4
♡ A 6                 ♡ 10
◇ A 9 8 3 2           ◇ K Q 7 5 4
♣ K Q                 ♣ 9 6 3 2
          ♠ J
          ♡ Q J 9 7 5 2
          ◇ J 10
          ♣ A 10 8 4
```

When South, Dick Freeman, one of the former Quiz Kids (can anyone remember that far back?) played this hand at a National Championships in Montreal, he won the opening lead and restrained himself from leading a trump at Trick 2.

Do you see what would have happened? West would win the ace, cash the ♣Q, and underlead his ◇A to East and get a club ruff. Down one. Freeman saw all this coming and led a diamond at Trick 2 — while the clubs were blocked. Now the defense was helpless as Freeman had removed East's diamond entry prematurely and no ruff was available. So, you see, sometimes the only way to avoid a ruff is not to draw trumps.

Is this a perverse game, or what?

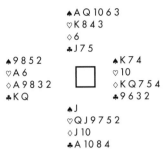

A sense of occasion

Which card do you lead from the 10-4-2? The normal lead is the 2, but there are times when leading the 10 is better. But as many-time World Champion Giorgio Belladonna might have pointed out, the following hand was not one of them.

Neither vul.

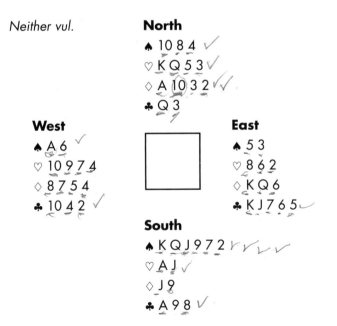

```
              North
              ♠ 10 8 4
              ♡ K Q 5 3
              ◇ A 10 3 2
              ♣ Q 3

West                          East
♠ A 6                         ♠ 5 3
♡ 10 9 7 4                    ♡ 8 6 2
◇ 8 7 5 4                     ◇ K Q 6
♣ 10 4 2                      ♣ K J 7 6 5

              South
              ♠ K Q J 9 7 2
              ♡ A J
              ◇ J 9
              ♣ A 9 8
```

West	North	East	South
			1♠
pass	2♢	pass	3♠
pass	4♠	all pass	

Opening lead: ♡10

When the dummy came down, Belladonna, playing in a World Pairs event, could see at a glance that this deal was not about making 4♠, this contract was about overtricks. He won the opening lead with the ace and played the ♠K, driving out West's ace.

West now shifted to a club, the ten to be exact. This was going to cost. Giorgio covered with the queen and captured the king. He cashed the ♡J, entered dummy with a spade and discarded a club and the ◇J on the K-Q of hearts.

Then came the parade of spades reducing all hands to two cards. Dummy remained with the A-10 of diamonds, Giorgio had two minor-suit nines, and poor East was squeezed in the minors because of that ♣10 play. He had the ◇K-Q and the ♣J left. He eventually discarded the ♣J hoping his partner had the nine. No such luck. Belladonna took the last two tricks with the ♣9 and the ◇A. Making six for a top score.

They tell a story about Giorgio when he was first learning English and found himself in a New York department store. He managed to ask one of the clerks where the restroom was. She pointed to the rear of the store and said, 'Near the escalator.' Giorgio replied, 'No later, right now!'

Hell hath no fury...

I'm afraid that after you look at the bidding you won't read the rest. Patience: a story goes with it. (You don't have to see the East-West hands.)

Both vul.

North
- ♠ K 5
- ♡ A 9 4 3
- ◇ A K 8
- ♣ K Q 7 5

South
- ♠ A Q J 10 9 8 6 4
- ♡ 2
- ◇ 10 7 5 3
- ♣ —

South	North
2♠[1]	4NT
5◇	5NT
6◇[2]	6NT
7♠[3]	pass

1. Meant as a strong two!
2. Counting the club void as a king.
3. Beyond comment.

West doubled and led the ♣A.

The hand is from a San Francisco Regional and it was bid by a pair of ladies who were aggravated with each other even before the hand started. Neither was a very good player, but the bidding diagram (the only 7-point strong two-bid ever made) makes that rather obvious.

When South showed only one ace to North's Blackwood query, North didn't believe her and bid 5NT anyway. (5NT after 4NT, besides being a king-ask, is supposed to guarantee joint possession of all four aces). After South showed a king (she counted the club void as a king!), North decided to believe that they were off an ace and signed off at 6NT. South couldn't stand that contract and bid 7♠. West had heard enough and doubled expecting the ♣A to cash.

When North saw the ♣A hit the table, she screamed at South, 'Don't you think I know what I'm doing?' But after ruffing, South shouted right back, 'And don't you think I know what I'm doing?' Making seven.

Of course this was the only pair who 'scientifically' bid and made seven spades — doubled, no less.

Have you ever played against an opponent who more or less stared down his partner, willing him to make the desired lead?

The biter bit

Neither vul.

North
♠ 10 8 7 6
♡ 6
◇ Q 10 4 2
♣ K J 10 9

West
♠ K 5
♡ A 9 7 5
◇ K 9 8 7 5 3
♣ 5

East
♠ 3 2
♡ K Q J 10 8 4 3 2
◇ A J
♣ 2

South
♠ A Q J 9 4
♡ —
◇ 6
♣ A Q 8 7 6 4 3

West	North	East	South
		4♡	4♠
5♡	5♠	pass	pass
dbl	all pass		

Opening lead: ♣5

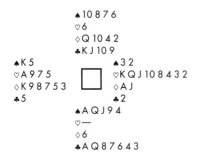

```
            ♠ 10 8 7 6
            ♡ 6
            ◇ Q 10 4 2
            ♣ K J 10 9
♠ K 5                        ♠ 3 2
♡ A 9 7 5        ┌──┐        ♡ K Q J 10 8 4 3 2
◇ K 9 8 7 5 3   │  │        ◇ A J
♣ 5             └──┘        ♣ 2
            ♠ A Q J 9 4
            ♡ —
            ◇ 6
            ♣ A Q 8 7 6 4 3
```

South happened to be playing against not one but two unethical players. He wasn't about to let this piece of good luck slip by quickly. South's unusual bidding had enabled him to stumble into a beautiful ice-cold contract without ever having mentioned his seven-card side suit. Most players would overcall clubs before spades, but South wanted to get that major in early. West clearly should not have doubled 5♠ holding four hearts to the ace. It was a moral certainty one opponent had a void. He should bid 6♡, which goes down only one. Now on to the play.

The club lead was won in dummy and it was apparent that each opponent had started with a singleton club and would want a club ruff when his partner got in. At Trick 2 the ♠10 rode to West's king. At this point East went into his act. He wanted a club return so badly he could taste it. He began to squirm and stare menacingly at West. In the meantime, West was trying to figure out how to get East in for a club ruff of his own.

West finally emerged from his trance by leading a low heart, much to East's obvious disgust. East played the ten, and South, wanting to see a bit more of this drama, discarded his singleton diamond, a loser in any case. But now it was West who started to squirm waiting for East to return a club. East, by now a total wreck, tried to cash the ◇A which South ruffed. South drew the last trump and claimed the balance. Both East and West, anxious to get at each other for not leading a club, failed to notice that no club ruff was available.

South never had so much fun in his life.

Do you mumble to yourself while you play bridge?   Read on.

*Loose lips
sink ships*

N-S vul.

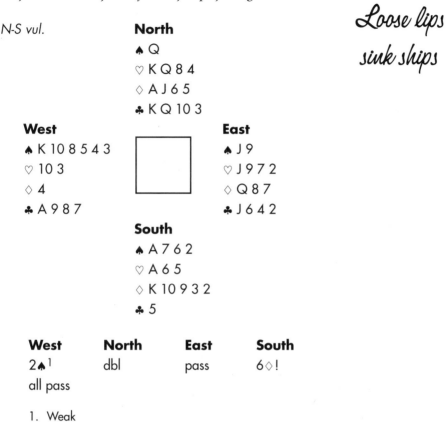

North
- ♠ Q
- ♡ K Q 8 4
- ◇ A J 6 5
- ♣ K Q 10 3

West
- ♠ K 10 8 5 4 3
- ♡ 10 3
- ◇ 4
- ♣ A 9 8 7

East
- ♠ J 9
- ♡ J 9 7 2
- ◇ Q 8 7
- ♣ J 6 4 2

South
- ♠ A 7 6 2
- ♡ A 6 5
- ◇ K 10 9 3 2
- ♣ 5

West	North	East	South
2♠[1]	dbl	pass	6◇!
all pass			

1. Weak

Opening lead: ♣A

One of the most amusing hands ever to emerge from the Hawaiian Regional was the above number.   No names included.

West had a normal enough Weak Two and South fell in love with her hand and that was that. After the opening lead of the ♣A, South's problem was the ◇Q. However, she received a rather fortuitous clue. Here's what happened. After cashing the club ace, West went into a long huddle and began mumbling to himself just loud enough for South to hear. 'I wonder what South has for that 6◇ bid. Surely she must have the K-Q of diamonds, the ace of hearts and the ace of spades.'

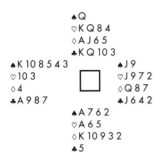

```
              ♠Q
              ♡KQ84
              ◇AJ65
              ♣KQ103
♠K108543               ♠J9
♡103          ┌────┐    ♡J972
◇4           │    │    ◇Q87
♣A987        └────┘    ♣J642
              ♠A762
              ♡A65
              ◇K10932
              ♣5
```

When South heard from West that she was supposed to have the ◇Q, it didn't take an Einstein to figure out who had it. When West finally shifted to a heart, South won in dummy, cashed the ◇A and led a diamond to the ten to wrap up her slam. Personally, I think this would have been a better story if West had the ◇Q! Of course South would have murdered him on the spot when he turned up with the queen, but would a jury of bridge players have found her guilty? Doubtful.

Too many bogeys

The World Par Bridge Tournament has been held infrequently. One reason is that the hands were so difficult almost no one could solve them. Just to give you an example...

Neither vul.

North

♠ Q 5 4
♡ Q 3 2
◇ 7 6 5
♣ K Q J 10

West

♠ 8 7
♡ 10 5 4
◇ J 8 3 2
♣ 7 6 4 2

East

♠ K 3 2
♡ K J 9
◇ Q 10 9
♣ A 8 5 3

South

♠ A J 10 9 6
♡ A 8 7 6
◇ A K 4
♣ 9

West	North	East	South
			1♠
pass	2♣	pass	2♡
pass	2♠	pass	4♠
all pass			

Opening lead: ♣2

In this deal North-South receive their bidding par if they arrive at a contract of 4♠. The defensive par is to defeat the contract with the mandated lead of the ♣2.

Written instructions are given to declarer when there is a defensive par and vice versa when it is a play par. This is to ensure that a pair 'earns' their par. On this deal East is told to win the ♣A and shift to the ◇10. South must win and is directed to lead the ♠J. East must duck to prevent the ♠Q from becoming an entry to the good clubs. South is now directed to lead the ♠10. Once again East must duck, sacrificing his king for the greater good of killing the club suit.

South is now directed to lead the ace of spades and a second high diamond. East must unblock the queen to avoid a throw-in. South exits with a diamond to West's jack and trumps West's diamond return. South is now instructed to lead a low heart and, in order to defeat the contract, West must play the ten lest South duck the trick into East, forcing either a club return or a heart from the king.

This is quite a defensive par. East must win the first club, duck two rounds of spades sacrificing his king, unblock the ◇Q to avoid a throw-in and even if East does all of that, West still has to play the ♡10 when the suit is first led.

No wonder they don't hold this contest very often.

The average bridge player wonders what an expert thinks about when the dummy comes down. Okay, here are a couple of secrets. If the contract looks near-hopeless, the expert places the opposing cards where he needs them to be to make the contract. If the contract looks relatively easy, he asks himself what can go wrong and what, if anything, he can do about it. With that as a guide, can you work out the best play for 3NT on these hands?

Both vul.

North
- ♠ J 6 5 2
- ♡ A 3
- ◇ Q J 10 8 3
- ♣ A 5

South
- ♠ A 10
- ♡ K Q 7 4
- ◇ 9 6 5
- ♣ K Q 6 2

West	North	East	South
			1♣
pass	1◇	pass	1♡
pass	1♠	pass	1NT
pass	3NT	all pass	

Opening lead: ♠7

East plays the king of spades, and the ball is in your court. What is your plan?

Diamonds have to be set up before the opponents can set up three spade tricks. If spades are 4-3 and West has the queen, which is apparent from East's play of the king, the hand cannot be defeated whether or not you win the first spade. However, if spades are 5-2 and the diamond honors are divided, the hand can be defeated if you take the ♠A. East can win the first diamond and return a spade, allowing West to win the queen and drive out the jack. When West gets in with the other diamond honor, he has the setting trick in spades.

But if you duck the first trick, win the second, and now knock out a diamond honor, you are home free. If East wins the trick he has no spade to return and the diamonds can be easily established. So, in order to protect against 5-2 spades and split diamond honors, duck the opening lead. See how easy it is.

The full deal:

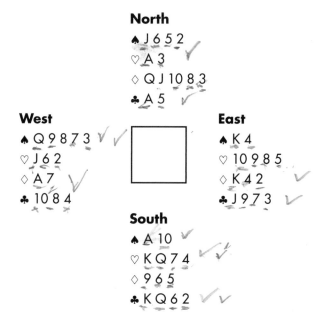

North
♠ J 6 5 2
♡ A 3
◇ Q J 10 8 3
♣ A 5

West
♠ Q 9 8 7 3
♡ J 6 2
◇ A 7
♣ 10 8 4

East
♠ K 4
♡ 10 9 8 5
◇ K 4 2
♣ J 9 7 3

South
♠ A 10
♡ K Q 7 4
◇ 9 6 5
♣ K Q 6 2

A delicate deal

True story. There I was in a local deli minding my own business when boom, Bernie Bernheim, a friend, plunks this napkin down in my face with four hands neatly penciled in. He tells me he played the deal in a local tournament the week before partnered by his wife Anne and I should take a look. I take a look. Bernie was South.

Both vul.

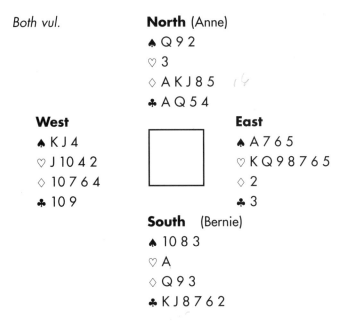

North (Anne)
- ♠ Q 9 2
- ♡ 3
- ◇ A K J 8 5
- ♣ A Q 5 4

West
- ♠ K J 4
- ♡ J 10 4 2
- ◇ 10 7 6 4
- ♣ 10 9

East
- ♠ A 7 6 5
- ♡ K Q 9 8 7 6 5
- ◇ 2
- ♣ 3

South (Bernie)
- ♠ 10 8 3
- ♡ A
- ◇ Q 9 3
- ♣ K J 8 7 6 2

The bidding is going to be hard to digest, but this is what happened. Anne, North, opened 1◇ and East overcalled 2♡. Bernie didn't think he was strong enough to bid 3♣ so he compromised with 2♠! West bid 2NT, which was explained as asking East for a singleton. Anne raised to 3♠ and East bid 4♣, his stronger singleton. Bernie passed discreetly and West corrected to 4♡, which was passed around to Bernie. Bernie bid 4♠! What else? East doubled and 4♠ doubled became the final contract.

West decided to lead a club which Bernie won in his hand to lead a low spade. West shot up with the king and led a club which East ruffed. Two tricks lost.

East shifted to a heart to Bernie's ace and he led a

second spade to the nine and ace. (East should have ducked). East returned a heart which Bernie ruffed in his hand. Next, he crossed to dummy with a diamond and played the ♠Q drawing the two remaining trumps. That's all she wrote. Bernie had the rest with high diamonds and high clubs. Way to go Bernie.

When the following deal was played in the Life Masters' Pairs only one declarer managed to go down. Don't tell me you will be the second!

Way to go — down!

North
♠ K 8 7 6
♡ K Q 9 3
◇ 10 4
♣ 7 6 5

South
♠ A 10 9 5
♡ A J 7
◇ Q 3 2
♣ A K 4

With no interference bidding you arrive in 4♠ and the lead is the ♣Q. How would you play it?

There are so many ways to make this hand (spades are 3-2), that it is almost impossible to go down. Sorry, in bridge nothing is impossible. This is how it happened.

Declarer won the opening lead and played the ace and five of spades to the king, leaving one high trump outstanding, and began to run his hearts. He didn't get very far. East, the player with the high trump, ruffed the third heart and returned a club. Dummy now had a winning heart, declarer a losing club and, you guessed it, declarer had no entry to dummy's heart. Declarer couldn't get to the heart because he had cleverly left himself the 10-9 of spades while dummy had the 8-7. When he exited with a diamond, the defenders cashed two diamonds and a club. Down one.

Here is the full deal:

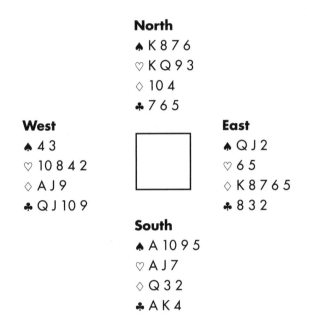

North
♠ K 8 7 6
♡ K Q 9 3
◇ 10 4
♣ 7 6 5

West
♠ 4 3
♡ 10 8 4 2
◇ A J 9
♣ Q J 10 9

East
♠ Q J 2
♡ 6 5
◇ K 8 7 6 5
♣ 8 3 2

South
♠ A 10 9 5
♡ A J 7
◇ Q 3 2
♣ A K 4

So how should the hand be played? There are several possibilities — here are two:

(1) Play the ace-king and a third spade. Now it is easy enough to discard a losing club on a heart without anybody ruffing.

(2) Cash the ♠A and run the ♠9. Assuming it loses, win the club return, draw the last trump and play hearts.

Why are so many bridge books aimed at preventing you from making a mistake, rather than being devoted to preventing partner from making a mistake? Everyone knows that most mistakes at the bridge table are made by partner.

It's OK,
I've got
you covered

N-S vul.

North
♠ K 10 9 2
♡ Q 3 2
♢ J 6 5
♣ K 9 3

West
♠ A 8 6 3
♡ 6 4
♢ A Q 4 2
♣ Q 4 2

East
♠ Q J 7
♡ J 5
♢ K 9 8 7 3
♣ 10 8 5

South
♠ 5 4
♡ A K 10 9 8 7
♢ 10
♣ A J 7 6

West	North	East	South
1♢	pass	2♢	2♡
pass	3♡	pass	4♡
all pass			

Opening lead: ♢ A

Assume you are West playing with a weaker player than yourself. This should be easy, because everyone you play with is weaker than you. At Trick 2 you continue with a diamond, which South ruffs. He continues with the ♡ A and a heart to the queen dropping partner's jack (are you counting?) and ruffs dummy's last diamond. At this point you know (or should know) that South started with six hearts and one diamond. Declarer continues with a spade to the king as you play low and now a spade from dummy, partner

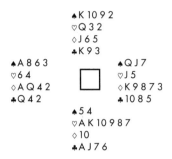

North
♠ K 10 9 2
♡ Q 3 2
◊ J 6 5
♣ K 9 3

West
♠ A 8 6 3
♡ 6 4
◊ A Q 4 2
♣ Q 4 2

East
♠ Q J 7
♡ J 5
◊ K 9 8 7 3
♣ 10 8 5

South
♠ 5 4
♡ A K 10 9 8 7
◊ 10
♣ A J 7 6

playing the jack. Which spade do you play?

'Are you joking?' you may ask. 'Why wouldn't I just play low?' That's exactly what West did, and how he rued the play. His partner shifted to a low club, declarer played low and West was forced to play the queen. Goodbye club trick, goodbye contract. What West should have done is overtake partner's jack and play another spade to partner's queen. Yes, South trumps and the ♠ 10 in dummy is now high, but so what?

Declarer has four clubs (remember, West is counting and can tell from the way spades are being played that declarer has a small doubleton, leaving him with four clubs) and one club discard on a spade won't help. If West overtakes and returns a spade, the queen of clubs will be the setting trick.

That's what somebody should write a book about: How to save partner from himself. Not a bad title actually.

Art, not science

When holding equal honors as declarer, do you know which one to lead to encourage a mistake? It's actually an art form.

Both vul.

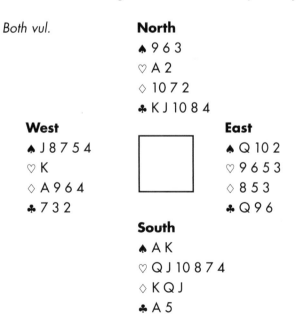

North
♠ 9 6 3
♡ A 2
◊ 10 7 2
♣ K J 10 8 4

West
♠ J 8 7 5 4
♡ K
◊ A 9 6 4
♣ 7 3 2

East
♠ Q 10 2
♡ 9 6 5 3
◊ 8 5 3
♣ Q 9 6

South
♠ A K
♡ Q J 10 8 7 4
◊ K Q J
♣ A 5

West	North	East	South
			2♣[1]
pass	3♣	pass	3♡
pass	4♡	pass	4NT
pass	5◇	pass	6♡
all pass			

1. Strong and artificial

North-South were not playing Keycard Blackwood. If they were, they would have discovered that two of the five keycards were missing (the king of the agreed suit counts as a keycard).

West, thinking he had a likely trump trick sitting in back of the original heart bidder, led the ace and another diamond. South took stock. His only chance was to find the singleton or doubleton king of hearts with West, but he had to be sure which it was if West played the king when South led an honor. Much depends upon which honor South elects to lead.

If South leads the jack or queen and West covers, South can't be sure whether the king is singleton or doubleton, as West might cover with K-x. However, if the ten is led and West covers, there is a far greater chance that the king is singleton. Not many defenders would be clever enough to cover with K-9 doubleton. So the ten was led and when West played the king, South played for the king to be a singleton, won the ace and led a low heart to the eight to bag the slam.

The golden rule for declarer with equal honors: If you want an honor covered, lead the higher or highest equal; if you don't want an honor covered, lead the second or third highest equal.

Overbidders had better be good declarers... or else.

A glimmer of hope

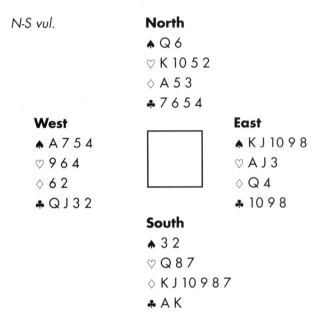

N-S vul.

North
- ♠ Q 6
- ♡ K 10 5 2
- ◇ A 5 3
- ♣ 7 6 5 4

West
- ♠ A 7 5 4
- ♡ 9 6 4
- ◇ 6 2
- ♣ Q J 3 2

East
- ♠ K J 10 9 8
- ♡ A J 3
- ◇ Q 4
- ♣ 10 9 8

South
- ♠ 3 2
- ♡ Q 8 7
- ◇ K J 10 9 8 7
- ♣ A K

West	North	East	South
		1♠	2◇
2♠	3◇	pass	4◇
all pass			

Opening lead: ♠A

The 4◇ bid was from outer space. Surely there could be no game facing a hand that could only make a single raise. On to the play.

West continued with a spade to East's king and East exited with the ♣10.

South now had to limit his heart losers to one trick. Not so easy, as East is likely to have the ♡AJ(x) on the bidding and the play so far. See any hope?

South saw hope. He won the club shift, cashed the ◇K, cashed a second club and crossed to dummy with the ◇A, felling the queen, thank you very much, and ruffed a club, stripping East of clubs. The table was set: South led a low heart to the king. East was obliged to win and was left with the guarded jacks of hearts and spades. Either return is fatal. East actually led a low heart, but South floated that around to the ten in dummy. Had East led a spade, South can ruff in dummy and toss off his losing eight of hearts.

The key to the play was partially stripping the clubs before leading a heart to the king. After all, when you are pretty sure that both the ace and the jack are hovering over the K-10-x and you have Q-x-x without the nine, your options are limited.

Lest there be any doubt that Helen Sobel was one of the greatest players of all time, take a look at her defense with the West hand here, partnered by the legendary Charles Goren.

The female of the species

E-W vul.

North
♠ A K 8 2
♡ A K 4 2
◇ Q 5
♣ 6 5 3

West (Sobel)
♠ 6 5
♡ J 8 6
◇ A K J 8 6 3
♣ A 9

East (Goren)
♠ 10 9 4 3
♡ 10 3
◇ 9 2
♣ K J 10 7 2

South
♠ Q J 7
♡ Q 9 7 5
◇ 10 7 4
♣ Q 8 4

West	North	East	South
1◇	dbl	pass	1♡
pass	2♡	all pass	

Opening lead: ◇A

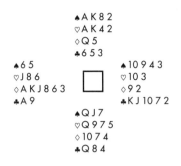

```
              ♠ A K 8 2
              ♡ A K 4 2
              ◇ Q 5
              ♣ 6 5 3
♠ 6 5                      ♠ 10 9 4 3
♡ J 8 6        ┌──┐        ♡ 10 3
◇ A K J 8 6 3  │  │        ◇ 9 2
♣ A 9          └──┘        ♣ K J 10 7 2
              ♠ Q J 7
              ♡ Q 9 7 5
              ◇ 10 7 4
              ♣ Q 8 4
```

Helen began with three rounds of diamonds, dummy pitching a club and Goren throwing off the ♣7. Without hesitation Sobel switched to the nine of clubs! Goren won the king, returned a club to Helen's ace, and ruffed the fourth round of diamonds (dummy discarding a spade) with the ♡10 promoting Helen's ♡J to the setting trick. Nice 'D'.

Someone once asked Helen what it felt like playing with a great expert. She replied: 'Ask Charlie.'

Hard to believe, but...

Terence Reese, one of the world's great player-writers, once posed this play problem to his readers:

Both vul.

North

♠ 4 3 2
♡ Q 9
◇ 10 8 6 4
♣ A K Q 9

South

♠ A 10 8 7 5
♡ A 5 3
◇ A
♣ J 7 6 2

West	North	East	South
			1 ♠
pass	2 ♣	pass	3 ♣
pass	3 ♠	pass	4 ♠
all pass			

Opening lead: ♠6

Notice that North is duty-bound to give three-card major suit support, regardless of the quality of those three cards.

On to the play. East plays the ♠Q at Trick 1. Say you duck and East continues with the ♠K which you win, West following with the nine. How do you continue? Do not come home lame, the hand is cold!

This may not look like a dummy reversal, but it is. Cash the ◇A, cross to a club and ruff a diamond; back to a club, ruff another diamond and back to a club to ruff dummy's last diamond. If nobody has trumped anything yet with the good ♠J, play a fourth high club. If that lives, you have ten tricks: ♠A, ♡A, ◇A, four clubs and three diamond ruffs. And what if a defender ruffs one of your club winners? Fine, then you have a trump in dummy to handle your heart loser.

The full deal:

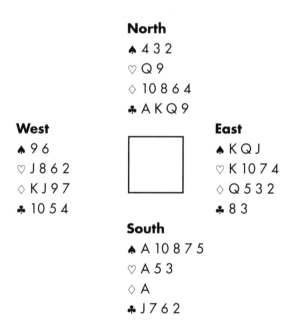

North
♠ 4 3 2
♡ Q 9
◇ 10 8 6 4
♣ A K Q 9

West
♠ 9 6
♡ J 8 6 2
◇ K J 9 7
♣ 10 5 4

East
♠ K Q J
♡ K 10 7 4
◇ Q 5 3 2
♣ 8 3

South
♠ A 10 8 7 5
♡ A 5 3
◇ A
♣ J 7 6 2

The player who went down won the second spade and led a low heart to the queen thinking that even if East had the king, West surely had the ♠J and a heart could be trumped in dummy. Surprise! East had both the ♠J and the ♡K. He cashed the ♠J upon winning the heart and South wound up one trick short.

It is safer to trump three diamonds in the closed hand than one heart in dummy because the lead does not have to be surrendered while you are trumping diamonds.

A fishy tale

One of the best loved of American post-war bridge experts was Harry 'Fishy' Fishbein of New York City. Fishy always wore a different colored beret each day at tournaments and always had a good story ready for anyone who would listen. Get a load of this defensive play he made in the West seat.

Neither vul.

North
♠ J 7 6 2
♡ Q J 3
◇ K 9 3
♣ 10 6 3

West (Fishy)
♠ Q 4
♡ 6 5 4
◇ A Q J 10 6 2
♣ Q 5

East
♠ 10 3
♡ 10 9
◇ 8 7 5 4
♣ A K 9 7 2

South
♠ A K 9 8 5
♡ A K 8 7 2
◇ —
♣ J 8 4

West	North	East	South
			1♠
2◇	2♠	3♣	4♡
pass	4♠	all pass	

Opening lead: ♣Q

Fishbein continued a club to East's king and when East played the ♣A, what do you think Fishy discarded? Yup, you've got it. He unloaded the ◊A! The idea was to jolt partner into playing a fourth round of clubs to promote the ♠Q to the setting trick. Fishy knew that a club would beat 4♠, but a diamond shift might not. Was he ever right.

A lesser player might have discarded the deuce of diamonds to tell the same story, but such a 'peasant-like' discard never crossed Fishy's mind. He wanted to give his partner a discard he wouldn't forget.

B.J Becker, one of the greatest bridge players of all time, once put together a collection of his favorite hands and put them in an attractive pocketbook entitled Becker on Bridge. *What follows is my favorite hand from that book.*

Pinochle deck

Neither vul.

North
♠ 3 2
♡ Q 6 3
◊ Q 3 2
♣ K Q J 10 6

West
♠ 6 5
♡ 9 8 7
◊ 10 9 8 7
♣ 5 4 3 2

East
♠ J 4
♡ K J 10 2
◊ K J 6
♣ A 9 8 7

South
♠ A 10 K Q 9 8 7
♡ A 5 4
◊ A 5 4
♣ —

West	North	East	South
		1♣	2♣
pass	3NT	pass	6♠
all pass			

Opening lead: ♣2

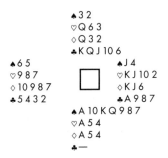

```
            ♠ 3 2
            ♡ Q 6 3
            ◇ Q 3 2
            ♣ K Q J 10 6
♠ 6 5                    ♠ J 4
♡ 9 8 7                  ♡ K J 10 2
◇ 10 9 8 7               ◇ K J 6
♣ 5 4 3 2                ♣ A 9 8 7
            ♠ A 10 K Q 9 8 7
            ♡ A 5 4
            ◇ A 5 4
            ♣ —
```

As B.J tells it, this South player named John hated bridge primarily because he had a passion for pinochle. Now pinochle is a crazy game which uses forty-eight cards out of a double deck; the nine is the lowest card in the game. Furthermore, the rank of the cards is similar to bridge except that after the ace, the ten is the next-highest card followed by the king, etc.

One day John was at the club and they needed him desperately for a bridge game. Reluctantly he consented and wound up with the great hand you see in the South seat. Naturally John sorted the hand as if he were playing pinochle, putting the ten next to the ace and wasted no time barging into 6♠ after his partner showed him a pretty good hand.

In the play John outdid himself. He ruffed East's ace of clubs and set about drawing trump by playing the ace and then the ten! Of course he thought that the ten was the next highest spade. East now made a surprise trick with the ♠J, but it was to cost him dearly. What could he lead? A club was certain death as was leading away from his red kings, allowing an entry to dummy's clubs. Slam made.

When last heard, John doesn't play pinochle any more. You can't tear him away from the bridge table.

I couldn't resist having a little fun in one of my classes. I have this trick deal that nobody ever gets right and I snuck it into the playing part of the lesson. You can't believe what happened.

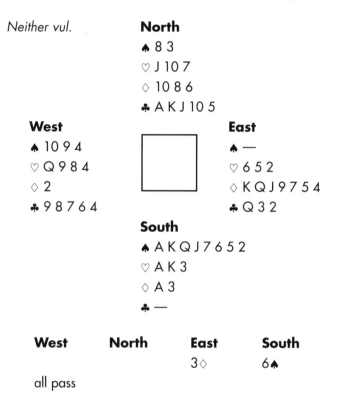

The best-laid plans

Neither vul.

North
♠ 8 3
♡ J 10 7
♢ 10 8 6
♣ A K J 10 5

West
♠ 10 9 4
♡ Q 9 8 4
♢ 2
♣ 9 8 7 6 4

East
♠ —
♡ 6 5 2
♢ K Q J 9 7 5 4
♣ Q 3 2

South
♠ A K Q J 7 6 5 2
♡ A K 3
♢ A 3
♣ —

West	North	East	South
		3♢	6♠

all pass

Opening lead: ♢ 2

In class we don't waste time on the bidding. The play's the thing. Before I tell you how to make 6♠, can you figure it out? Nobody in any of my classes could.

The trick is to get to dummy to use the A-K of clubs without crawling under the table. Here's how. Win the diamond opening lead and play the ace, king and deuce of spades. West must win the trick and has to lead a club or a heart. Either exit puts you in dummy where you can cash your club winners.

Although I never watch my students play a hand because it makes them nervous (and me apoplectic), I

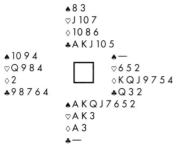

♠ 8 3
♡ J 10 7
◇ 10 8 6
♣ A K J 10 5

♠ 10 9 4　　　　♠ —
♡ Q 9 8 4　　　　♡ 6 5 2
◇ 2　　　　　　　◇ K Q J 9 7 5 4
♣ 9 8 7 6 4　　　♣ Q 3 2

♠ A K Q J 7 6 5 2
♡ A K 3
◇ A 3
♣ —

couldn't resisting watching this one at several tables. This is what happened:

At Table 1 declarer ducked the diamond opening lead and East shifted to a heart instead of giving partner a diamond ruff. No matter, declarer still had to lose a heart. Down one.

At Table 2 declarer won the diamond lead and led a low spade! West rose with the nine and led a heart, so declarer made the hand, winning the heart in dummy, and discarding a diamond on the ace of clubs, etc.

At Table 3 declarer won the opening lead and played the A-K of clubs from dummy discarding two red suit losers. This is clearly the best play if the defenders let you get away with it. 'What's the problem?' she asked as she tabled her cards. I stopped watching.

Vive le deux!

The following hand was played in Paris by Roger Trezel. It is something else.

Both vul.

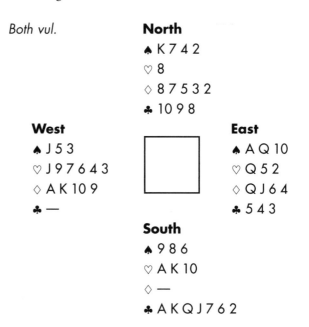

North
♠ K 7 4 2
♡ 8
◇ 8 7 5 3 2
♣ 10 9 8

West
♠ J 5 3
♡ J 9 7 6 4 3
◇ A K 10 9
♣ —

East
♠ A Q 10
♡ Q 5 2
◇ Q J 6 4
♣ 5 4 3

South
♠ 9 8 6
♡ A K 10
◇ —
♣ A K Q J 7 6 2

West	North	East	South
pass	pass	pass	1♣
1♡	pass	2♡	4♣
4♡	5♣	all pass	

Opening lead: ◇A

Trezel arrived at a great contract, but still had to make it. He suspected the ♠A was with East given the opening lead from a passed hand. Maybe you would like to try to make this contract looking at all four hands. I'll give you two days!

Trezel ruffed the opening lead high and led a low club (not the deuce, never the deuce) to dummy and ruffed another diamond high. He reentered dummy with a trump (not with the deuce), and ruffed a third diamond high. This was followed by the A-K of hearts and a heart ruff with dummy's last trump, and then by a fourth diamond ruff, again with a high trump.

At this point Trezel remained with his beloved deuce of clubs and three little spades. Dummy had K-x-x of spades and a winning diamond and East, the A-Q-10 of spades along with a high trump: the five! Trezel exited from his hand with a trump discarding a spade from the table. Poor East could no better than take his five of clubs and his ace of spades, but had to concede the last two tricks to dummy's ♠K and winning diamond. Wow!

The

winning

bet

Are you a gambler at heart? If so, which horse would you back in this 3NT contract with a spade lead, the defense or the declarer? Assume best defense, of course.

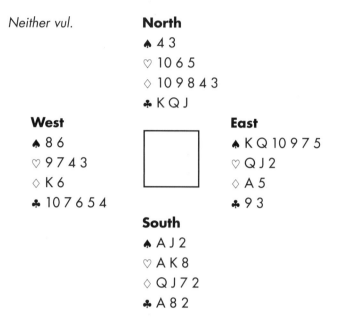

Neither vul.

North
- ♠ 4 3
- ♡ 10 6 5
- ◇ 10 9 8 4 3
- ♣ K Q J

West
- ♠ 8 6
- ♡ 9 7 4 3
- ◇ K 6
- ♣ 10 7 6 5 4

East
- ♠ K Q 10 9 7 5
- ♡ Q J 2
- ◇ A 5
- ♣ 9 3

South
- ♠ A J 2
- ♡ A K 8
- ◇ Q J 7 2
- ♣ A 8 2

West	North	East	South
	pass	1♠	dbl
pass	2◇	pass	2NT
pass	3NT	all pass	

Opening lead: ♠8

Doubling and then bidding notrump shows a stronger hand than a direct one notrump overcall. Anyway, who do you like?

If you chose the defense, you backed a winner. However, in order for the defense to prevail East must not play a spade honor at Trick 1; the nine will do just fine, thank you. South wins the jack and attacks diamonds. As long as West wins the first diamond and continues a spade driving out South's ace, declarer has no chance. East remains with winning spades and the ◇A for an entry.

If East plays a high spade at Trick 1, South ducks, wins

the spade continuation with the jack and attacks diamonds. Alas, West has no more spades when he gets in with the ◇K, and South has time to drive out the ◇A while retaining a spade stopper.

There's a defensive principle involved here. When declarer has two stoppers in the defenders' best suit (spades), and the defenders have two entries in declarer's best suit (diamonds), it behooves the defense to force declarer to win the first trick in the suit if possible. Here it is possible.

Something for everyone here: overtakes, ducking plays, frozen suits, the whole enchilada. In other words, a good lesson deal.

Deep freeze

Neither vul.

North
♠ 7 3 2
♡ 2
◇ A 8 7 6 4 3
♣ 9 6 5

West
♠ K Q J 8 6
♡ 5 4 3
◇ 9
♣ K 7 4 2

East
♠ A 10 9 5
♡ 10 9 6
◇ Q J 10
♣ J 10 8

South
♠ 4
♡ A K Q J 8 7
◇ K 5 2
♣ A Q 3

West	North	East	South
			1♡
1♠	pass	2♠	4♡
all pass			

Opening lead: ♠K

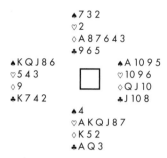

```
          ♠732
          ♡2
          ◇A 8 7 6 4 3
          ♣9 6 5
♠K Q J 8 6          ♠A 10 9 5
♡5 4 3             ♡10 9 6
◇9                 ◇Q J 10
♣K 7 4 2           ♣J 10 8
          ♠4
          ♡A K Q J 8 7
          ◇K 5 2
          ♣A Q 3
```

West overcame the temptation to lead his singleton diamond. Had he done that, there would have been no problem for declarer — and nothing to write about for me. On a diamond lead, South wins the king, draws trumps and ducks a diamond. East wins this trick, but the most East-West can take is a spade as the club losers go off on diamonds.

With the spade lead, at least there was hope. East, realizing the potential danger of dummy's diamonds, and knowing South had only one spade, overtook and shifted to the jack of clubs. South covered, West won and returned a club establishing a second trick for East. South was sunk — he still had to lose one more trick in each minor. Down one. Nice defense by East, but a major *error* by South.

When the ♣J is led, South can 'freeze' the club suit by playing the ace. If East has the king, the queen will take a trick later, but if West has it and East has the ten, the club suit is *frozen*. What exactly is a frozen (love that word) suit? It is a suit that neither side can lead without giving up a trick.

Say South wins the ♣A, draws trumps, discarding spades from the table, and plays the king and a diamond. When West shows out, the diamond is ducked into East who must attack clubs now to have any chance.

However, if East leads the ten, South covers, West wins, but dummy's nine is high. If East leads the eight, South ducks, West wins the king, and South's queen is high. It pays to remember that club position. When you are the declarer and this comes up, you can 'freeze the suit' by playing the ace.

The following hand might just be the best-played hand of all time. It was supposedly played by a seventeen-year-old from Indonesia, Oscar Irawan. After you read how he played it, you may understand why I am a bit skeptical.

Beyond belief?

Both vul.

North
♠ 6 4 3
♡ —
◇ 10 9 8 5 4 2
♣ 10 9 6 3

West
♠ —
♡ K Q J 10 7 6 4 3 2
◇ Q J
♣ K Q

East
♠ Q 10 8 7
♡ A 9 8 5
◇ 7 6 3
♣ 8 4

South
♠ A K J 9 5 2
♡ —
◇ A K
♣ A J 7 5 2

West	North	East	South
	pass	pass	2♠
4♡	4♠	pass	5♣
pass	5♠	pass	6♠
dbl	all pass		

Opening lead: ♡K

You might want to try to make this contract looking at all four hands. Here's how Oscar played it looking at only two.

He ruffed the opening lead in dummy with the six and underruffed with the five! At Trick 2 he led a spade to the nine. Not a bad start. Next he cashed the A-K of diamonds, felling West's Q-J, and exited with ace and a club to West.

West only had hearts left and when he led one, declarer ruffed in dummy with the four (dummy's last trump) and underruffed with the deuce in his hand. That was Oscar's

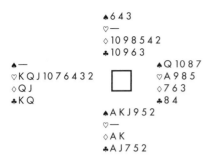

second underruff. There are many people who have played their whole life never having underruffed once!

With the lead in dummy, Oscar played high diamonds discarding clubs until East ruffed. Whenever East ruffs, South overruffs, draws trumps and has the balance. If East refuses to ruff, Oscar takes the last three tricks with the A-K-J of spades hovering over East's Q-10-8.

So, do you believe it?

Writers' choice

In the mid-sixties a book came out entitled Bridge Writers' Choice. *In this book each member of the IBPA (International Bridge Press Association) contributed their favorite deal. This one is entitled 'A Wonderful Sequence' and was written by Leon Sapire of South Africa. The deal comes from a tournament in Cape Town and is one that brought gasps from the kibitzers. North was Sam Kagan, South Bennie Saltzstein, both veteran players.*

N-S vul.

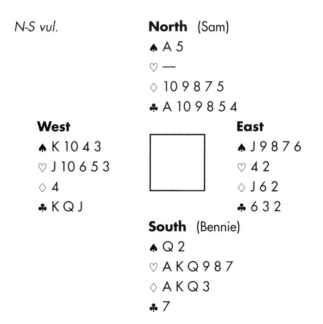

West	North	East	South
			1◇[1]
pass	1♡[2]	pass	3♣[3]
pass	4♣[4]	pass	4♡[5]
pass	6♣[6]	pass	6♡[7]
dbl	7◇[8]	pass	pass[9]
all pass			

1. I had better prepare a reverse to show a strong hand.

2. Surely we will play in six or seven diamonds and I don't want them sacrificing in hearts.

3. Wonderful — partner has hearts so I must stop the opponents from finding a club sacrifice. (Great minds think alike.)

4. Might as well set the trump suit; I like clubs a little more than diamonds.

5. Time to show my true colors.

6. Enough monkeying around.

7. Partner must have gone mad!

8. Partner must have gone mad!

9. I've had it with this sequence and this partner!

Opening lead: ♣K

Bennie won the ace, crossed to a trump, ruffed a low heart and then played two more diamonds, West shedding spades. The AKQ of hearts followed, dummy discarding clubs, and a heart was ruffed with dummy's last trump setting up Bennie's long heart. A club was ruffed in the closed hand with South's last trump and Bennie was down to a good heart and the Q-2 of spades. Dummy had the ♠A-5 and the ♣10. And West, what about West?

Don't look now, but West has the ♠K-10 and the ♣Q. When South plays his winning heart, West has to discard a spade, dummy throws its club and South takes the last two spade tricks. What can one say other than it was beautiful bidding?

Bellissimo!

Of all the hands the great Giorgio Belladonna has ever played, the one coming up is perhaps the most famous.

N-S vul.

North
♠ 7 6 5 2
♡ K 6 2
◇ J 6 3
♣ K Q 3

West
♠ K J 9 4
♡ Q J 5 4
◇ 10 4
♣ 10 5 2

East
♠ 8 3
♡ 10 8
◇ 5 2
♣ A J 9 8 7 6 4

South
♠ A Q 10
♡ A 9 7 3
◇ A K Q 9 8 7
♣ —

West	North	East	South
		4♣	5♣
pass	5NT	pass	6◇
all pass			

Opening lead: ♣10

Bidding usually gets a bit fuzzy after a four-level preempt. Belladonna had such a good hand he feared doubling lest partner pass and some slam would be missed. As a result he made a questionable cuebid. North's 5NT was supposed to show club strength and Belladonna had no trouble bidding 6◇. Now all he had to do was make it.

Notice that both spade honors are offside and hearts don't break. West, correctly thinking there was club strengh in the dummy, led the ♣10 instead of the more conventional low from three in partner's suit. Belladonna covered with the queen and ruffed East's ace. He continued with three rounds of diamonds ending in dummy, both defenders pitching clubs. Now Giorgio cashed the ♣K discarding the ♠10, and ruffed a club, West pitching a spade. This was the seven-card ending when Belladonna elected to play his last trump.

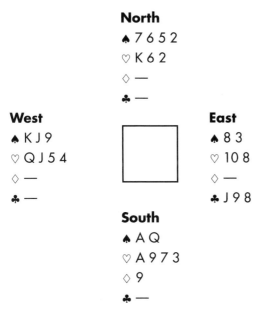

North
♠ 7 6 5 2
♡ K 6 2
◇ —
♣ —

West
♠ K J 9
♡ Q J 5 4
◇ —
♣ —

East
♠ 8 3
♡ 10 8
◇ —
♣ J 9 8

South
♠ A Q
♡ A 9 7 3
◇ 9
♣ —

On the ◇9, West discarded a heart. If he discards a spade, Belladonna plays the A-Q of spades and sets up two spade winners in dummy. However, the heart discard didn't help either. Belladonna continued with the king, ace and another heart throwing West in, setting up his long heart, and forcing a spade return into his A-Q all in one fell swoop.

Somehow Belladonna had wormed two extra tricks out of this ending. *Bravo* Giorgio.

Back from the dead

When partner makes an 'unlucky' lead (what else is new?), you may have to turn somersaults to get back to par.

Neither vul.

North
♠ A 3
♡ K Q 6
◇ K 7 2
♣ K J 9 7 3

West
♠ J 9 2
♡ J 8 5 4 3
◇ 10 8 3
♣ 8 2

East
♠ Q 5 4
♡ A 9 2
◇ A Q J 5
♣ A 10 4

South
♠ K 10 8 7 6
♡ 10 7
◇ 9 6 4
♣ Q 6 5

West	North	East	South
	1NT	dbl	pass
2♡	pass	pass	2♠
all pass			

Opening lead: ♣8

South didn't bid 2♠ directly over the double because he didn't mind playing 1NT doubled. However, when West ran to 2♡ and North passed, 2♠ looked right. Had West led the ◇10, this hand would have been over in seconds. The defenders would have collected three quick diamonds, two aces and a trump trick before South could rev up his engines. Down one. However, with the club lead there were big problems for the defenders — how to get those diamond tricks before they evaporated on clubs?

East won the opening lead and returned the suit hoping against hope that West had led a singleton club. No luck there. South won the club return with the queen and tried to draw trumps as quickly as possible. He led a spade to the ace and East came up with a brilliancy. He unblocked the ♠Q! East reasoned that South could not have six spades (he would have bid them one round earlier) and if he had ♠KJxxx, there was no hope. However, if declarer had the K10xxx of spades and partner Jxx, South could not prevent West from getting in if he unblocked. East actually needed three miracles for this play to work:

1) West must have the ♠J

2) West must have the ◊10

3) West must lead the ◊10 upon getting in with the ♠J.

The first two existed and West came through with number three. Down one. Nice!

Many years ago in Los Angeles there lived a young bridge wannabe named Patti. She aspired to be a top player and wanted to play with and learn from the best. One evening she was playing with Alex, a local expert, in a duplicate game. She and Alex arrived at 7♠ on these two hands:

Sleight of hand

North (Patti)
♠ 8 6 4 2
♡ K Q 3 2
◊ A 4
♣ Q J 6

☐

South (Alex)
♠ A K J 10
♡ A 5
◊ K Q J 7
♣ A K 8

♠ 8 6 4 2
♡ K Q 3 2
◊ A 4
♣ Q J 6

♠ A K J 10
♡ A 5
◊ K Q J 7
♣ A K 8

Alex won the opening heart lead in his hand and played the ♠A hoping the queen would drop. When it didn't, his plan was to cross to dummy and take a spade finesse... but first, he played the ♣K.

Keep in mind that he played the ♣K immediately after he played the ♠A. To West it looked for all the world like the ♠K. As West had Q-x of spades, she had pulled the queen out to follow suit when to her horror she realized she was following to the ♣K. She tried to pull the ♠Q back, but it was too late.

Everyone had seen it and Alex made his grand by playing the ♠K next.

To say Patti was impressed would be an understatement. She was determined to make the same play even if it took her a lifetime of waiting. It only took two years. Patti, playing with a different partner, arrived in 7♡ on these two hands with a spade lead.

North (new partner)
♠ 8 7
♡ 9 4 3 2
◊ Q 10 8 7
♣ A K Q

South (Patti)
♠ A K Q
♡ A K J 10
◊ A K J 5
♣ 9 7

Patti was so ready for the play that Alex taught her that she already had the ◊K tucked behind the ♡A so it could be played in perfect tempo. It was just like a dream. She won the opening lead and played the A♡ followed by the ◊K in perfect tempo. Alex would have been so proud. Sure enough, West played a small heart. Patti mentioned that she was leading a diamond. West said, 'I know; I don't have any'.

P.S. The ♡Q was doubleton onside!

When declarer is playing 3NT with eight sure tricks plus a possibly wide open suit, he does best to try to steal a ninth trick early. The defense, on the other hand, does best to try to count declarer's tricks as soon as possible to prevent any 'stealing'! What follows is an example of this battle of wits.

Caught stealing

E-W vul.

North
♠ A J 4
♡ 10 8 5 4 3
♢ A Q 5 4
♣ 2

West
♠ 10 8 7 2
♡ J 7 6
♢ 9 3
♣ 10 7 6 5

East
♠ Q 6 5
♡ A Q 9 2
♢ 6 2
♣ A J 4 3

South
♠ K 9 3
♡ K
♢ K J 10 8 7
♣ K Q 9 8

West	North	East	South
			1♢
pass	1♡	pass	2♣
pass	3♢	pass	3NT
all pass			

Opening lead: ♠2

Declarer played low from dummy and gobbled up East's queen. From declarer's point of view there are eight quick tricks and a ninth can be developed in clubs, but there is that 'hole' in hearts.

In order to conceal his trick count, declarer crossed to dummy with a spade, not a diamond (fearing the opponents would give each other count) and innocently led a club from

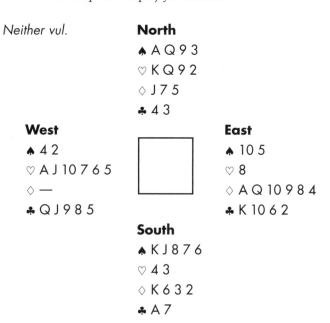

<table>
<tr><td></td><td>♠ A J 4
♡ 10 8 5 4 3
♢ A Q 5 4
♣ 2</td><td></td></tr>
<tr><td>♠ 10 8 7 2
♡ J 7 6
♢ 9 3
♣ 10 7 6 5</td><td></td><td>♠ Q 6 5
♡ A Q 9 2
♢ 6 2
♣ A J 4 3</td></tr>
<tr><td></td><td>♠ K 9 3
♡ K
♢ K J 10 8 7
♣ K Q 9 8</td><td></td></tr>
</table>

dummy. If East plays low, South has stolen a 9th trick. Even if East plays the ace, he has to be clever enough to switch to the ace and a heart. Can East be that clever?

Yes! Look at the hand from the East perspective. The bidding has presumably marked South with nine minor-suit cards. (Few bid this way with 4-4 in the minors). The opening lead has marked South with three spades, ergo a *singleton* heart. Counting tricks, East can count declarer for five diamonds and three spades so he knows that declarer is going for his ninth trick when a club is led from dummy. In other words, South is out there stealing!

If East thinks this out clearly, he will rise with the ♣A and play the ace and a heart collecting four heart tricks and a club, leaving South shaking his head.

Show me the way to go home

Preemptive bids are two-edged swords. They take away two or three levels of bidding space from the opponents and often drive them to hopeless contracts. On the other hand, they more or less blueprint the play for declarer.

Neither vul.

North
♠ A Q 9 3
♡ K Q 9 2
♢ J 7 5
♣ 4 3

West
♠ 4 2
♡ A J 10 7 6 5
♢ —
♣ Q J 9 8 5

East
♠ 10 5
♡ 8
♢ A Q 10 9 8 4
♣ K 10 6 2

South
♠ K J 8 7 6
♡ 4 3
♢ K 6 3 2
♣ A 7

West	North	East	South
		3◇ [1]	pass
pass	dbl	pass	4♠
all pass			

1. Six-card three-level preempts are the rage these days.
   Live with it.

Opening lead: ♣Q

West feared bidding 3♡, forcing, since it's usually a losing proposition to mess with a preempt with shortness in partner's suit unless you have a mountain.

South took stock. It didn't take much to work out from the lead that West was void in diamonds and that East had the ♣K. It was also pretty clear that if East had those honors, West must have the ♡A. Not a bad start. South won the opening lead, drew two rounds of trump ending in the closed hand and led a heart to the king, West ducking, and exited a club. Who should win this trick?

If *East* wins, he does best to exit with the ◇Q to declarer's king. A second heart goes to West's ace who gets out with the ♡J to dummy's queen, South shedding a diamond. Dummy plays the ♡9, declarer making the key play of discarding a second diamond, as West wins the ten. At this point West must lead a club or a heart, both losing plays: dummy ruffs and declarer discards his last diamond. Declarer winds up losing two hearts and one club, but no diamonds!

If *West* wins the club exit, the best he can do is cash the ♡A and exit with the ♡J to dummy's queen, South shedding a diamond. Now a diamond is led towards the king which East does best to duck. (If East wins, he either has to lead away from the ◇Q or give South a ruff-sluff.) After winning the ◇K, South crosses to dummy with a trump, and discards a diamond on the ♡9. West can do no better than win and get out with a club or a heart, allowing dummy to ruff as declarer gets rid of his last diamond. Once again East doesn't take a trick with the ◇A! *Olé.*

The year is 1935. The two top players of the time are Ely Culbertson and P. Hal Sims. There is a power struggle to see who can captivate the public with the best bridge system. Culbertson has more devotees, but Sims' followers are more fanatical. Finally a challenge is issued by Culbertson. He is willing to take on any pair in the world in a 150 rubber marathon for sizable stakes. His partner will be his wife, Josephine. P. Hal Sims accepts the challenge and announces he will play with his wife, Dorothy. Never has a bridge match had a more spectacular build-up by the media. Here is one of the more famous hands from the match:

Neither vul.

North (Dorothy)
- ♠ K J 3
- ♡ 7
- ◇ A Q 7 4
- ♣ K Q 9 4 2

West (Josephine)
- ♠ A 5 4
- ♡ 8 4 3 2
- ◇ K 9 6
- ♣ A 10 7

East (Ely)
- ♠ Q 10 7 6
- ♡ 10 5
- ◇ J 10 5 3 2
- ♣ 6 3

South (P. Hal)
- ♠ 9 8 2
- ♡ A K Q J 9 6
- ◇ 8
- ♣ J 8 5

West	North	East	South
pass	1♣	pass	1♡
pass	2◇	pass	3♡
pass	3NT	pass	4♡
all pass			

Opening lead: ♠4

P. Hal would have been better advised to play 3NT with his running heart suit, but he probably figured either contract would be cold and he wanted to get his 100 honors on the score sheet.

Josephine got off to the great lead of a low spade and Sims stuck in the jack which lost to the queen, Ely exiting with a trump. Trumps were drawn and a club was led which Josephine won with the ace. At this point Mrs. Culbertson made a play which was to make practically every newspaper in the country; she led another low spade! P. Hal Sims had a reputation for smelling out cards and seldom went wrong in these situations. Yet he could not believe that Josephine had underled her ace of spades *twice* on the same hand, so he played low. Ely won the ten and returned a spade to Josephine's ace, the setting trick. The Culbertsons went on to win the match by 16, 130 points and Contract Bridge was here to stay.

As an aside, Sims was once playing in a tournament against two ladies and had to find the ◇ Q to make the hand. He applied some thought as well as his famous table presence, and finally he announced 'Neither one of you has it.' And sure enough it was on the floor under the table!

How bad is bad?

When you play bridge for money you dread picking up a lousy hand because you are pretty sure it's going to cost you. How would you like to pick up this one, with both sides vulnerable, no less?

♠ 10 5   ♡ 8 7 6 4   ◇ 10 9 5 3   ♣ 8 7 3

You sit there waiting to see what catastrophe is going to befall you and it's not long in coming.

Your LHO opens 3♠ and partner makes a takeout double. RHO passes and it's your turn. If you pass they will probably make 3♠ doubled which will cost you 730 points, maybe 930 if they make an overtrick. On the other hand, if you bid and they double, there is no way of knowing how big a number you may go for.

♠ 10 5
♡ 8 7 6 4
◇ 10 9 5 3
♣ 8 7 3

You screw up your courage and bid 4♡. LHO passes and now you have to sweat out what your RHO is going to do. Not so fast. Have you forgotten about your partner? You have to get by him as well. Not this time. Your partner gently lifts you to 6♡. Incredibly everyone passes and the ♠K is led.

Once you have recovered from the trauma of it all, you still have to play the hand. You can hardly wait to see what partner is going to put down. Well, here it is:

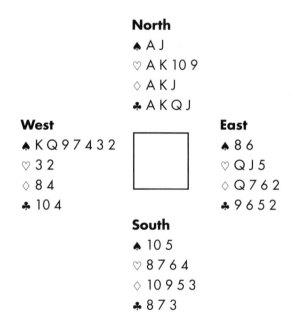

North
♠ A J
♡ A K 10 9
◇ A K J
♣ A K Q J

West
♠ K Q 9 7 4 3 2
♡ 3 2
◇ 8 4
♣ 10 4

East
♠ 8 6
♡ Q J 5
◇ Q 7 6 2
♣ 9 6 5 2

South
♠ 10 5
♡ 8 7 6 4
◇ 10 9 5 3
♣ 8 7 3

You can't really blame your partner for bidding again, can you? Be thankful he didn't bid seven! In any case you win the ♠A and play the A-K of hearts, both following — mercifully.

Next you play four rounds of clubs, discarding your spade and nobody trumps! Merrily you ruff a spade and exit with your last trump and guess what? East has to win and lead a diamond from the queen and you make the slam. You actually chalk up a vulnerable slam with your hand! Is bridge a great game, or what?

Pedro-Paulo (known as P.P.) Assumpcao, Brazilian World Team Olympiad Champion, contributed several tips on the play of the hand to the BOLS Bridge Tip Competition. This is one of them.

N-S vul.

North
♠ 10 6 5
♡ K 6 4
◇ 8 4 2
♣ K 9 8 2

West
♠ Q 9 4
♡ J 10 8
◇ Q J 5 3
♣ Q 10 4

East
♠ J 7
♡ A 9 7 3 2
◇ 10 6
♣ J 6 5 3

South
♠ A K 8 3 2
♡ Q 5
◇ A K 9 7
♣ A 7

West	North	East	South
			1♠
pass	1NT	pass	3◇
pass	3♠	pass	4♠
all pass			

Opening lead: ♡J

I'll let P.P describe the play: 'You win the opening lead with the queen, East signaling with the seven. You hope for a 3-2 trump break, but you may still need to look after your fourth diamond. The plan, therefore, must be to draw two rounds of trumps, give up a diamond and ruff a diamond if they break 4-2.

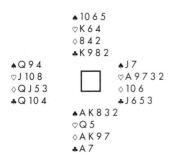

♠ 10 6 5
♡ K 6 4
◇ 8 4 2
♣ K 9 8 2

♠ Q 9 4
♡ J 10 8
◇ Q J 5 3
♣ Q 10 4

♠ J 7
♡ A 9 7 3 2
◇ 10 6
♣ J 6 5 3

♠ A K 8 3 2
♡ Q 5
◇ A K 9 7
♣ A 7

'The question is: What is the best timing? If you start with two top trumps and then give up a diamond, West will cash the ♠Q upon winning a diamond trick. No good. Suppose you begin with three rounds of diamonds. Still no good. West plays a fourth diamond and East overtrumps dummy.

'The answer is to start by *ducking a diamond.* Then you can cash the A-K of spades followed by the A-K of diamonds and a diamond ruff if necessary. And what if somebody trumps one of your high diamonds? No problem. Somebody is ruffing with the master trump (the high trump) and there will still be a trump in dummy to care for declarer's fourth diamond.'

I'd like to get my two cents worth in here. In this case dummy has low trump. If dummy has a high trump that can be used to ruff a fourth card in a side suit, the best timing is to cash the ace-king of the side suit, give up a trick in the suit and then if the side suit breaks 4-2, ruff the remaining loser high. The key to the way declarer attacks the side suit is dependent upon the size of dummy's highest trump.

Good bidding sees you agreeing on a trump suit before plunging into Blackwood, and even better bidding sees you using Keycard Blackwood after a suit has been agreed. Good defense sees you counting every hand. Enough said.

Rise and shine

Both vul.

North
- ♠ A K 4
- ♡ K J 9 2
- ◇ A K
- ♣ 8 6 5 2

West
- ♠ Q J 10 8 5
- ♡ 8 5
- ◇ Q 10 8 5 2
- ♣ J

East
- ♠ 9 6 2
- ♡ 7 3
- ◇ J 9 7 4
- ♣ K 10 9 7

South
- ♠ 7 3
- ♡ A Q 10 6 4
- ◇ 6 3
- ♣ A Q 4 3

West	North	East	South
			1♡
pass	3♣[1]	pass	4♣
pass	4NT	pass	5♠[2]
pass	5NT	pass	6♡[3]
all pass			

1. Forcing heart raise by agreement.
2. Two keycards plus the ♡Q.
3. No side kings.

Opening lead: ♠Q

From declarer's point of view, when there are losers in only one suit (clubs) and the hand can be stripped, clubs should be the last suit attacked. Declarer drew trumps, played the ace-king and ruffed a spade; then he played the ace-king of

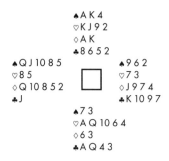

♠ A K 4
♡ K J 9 2
◇ A K
♣ 8 6 5 2

♠ Q J 10 8 5   ♠ 9 6 2
♡ 8 5   ♡ 7 3
◇ Q 10 8 5 2   ◇ J 9 7 4
♣ J   ♣ K 10 9 7

♠ 7 3
♡ A Q 10 6 4
◇ 6 3
♣ A Q 4 3

diamonds, setting the stage, and finally led a low club from dummy.

Take a good look at that club suit. A really good look. If East plays low on the club play from dummy, South can afford to play low as well, intending to take the finesse later. Look at what happens. West wins the jack, and has to give South a ruff and a sluff with a diamond or spade play. South ruffs in dummy, discarding a club and then takes the club finesse to bag the slam.

Not so fast. Enter East, 'the counter'. East had counted the South hand and knew his partner had a singleton club. If it was a small singleton and declarer had AQJx, there was no hope, but if the singleton was the jack or the queen, West could see what would happen if he played low. South would duck, partner would win and be endplayed. Instead, he played the king of clubs! After this diabolical defense, there was no way for South to avoid losing two club tricks.

Eight is not enough

What's the longest suit you have ever had and still let partner play the hand? How does AKQJ7532 grab you?

N-S vul.

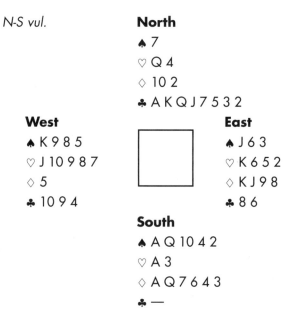

North
♠ 7
♡ Q 4
◇ 10 2
♣ A K Q J 7 5 3 2

West
♠ K 9 8 5
♡ J 10 9 8 7
◇ 5
♣ 10 9 4

East
♠ J 6 3
♡ K 6 5 2
◇ K J 9 8
♣ 8 6

South
♠ A Q 10 4 2
♡ A 3
◇ A Q 7 6 4 3
♣ —

West	North	East	South
			1♦
1♡!	2♣	2♡	2♠
pass	4♣	pass	4♦
pass	5♣	pass	5♦
all pass			

Opening lead: ♡J

The bidding requires a 'bit' of comment. I was North play-ing in a tournament with a relatively weak player who hap-pened to be the sponsor of the professional team I was on. West was angry over a previous result and would have over-called with an even weaker hand. As the bidding unfolded, I was trying to figure out how I could play this hand in clubs without taping my partner's mouth. After the 5♦ bid, (partner should have bid 4♠ over 4♣ to show me a 5-6 pat-tern) I feared we were off two heart tricks and passed 5♦. Besides, I didn't think my partner would let me play 6♣ (which makes). I could just feel it, not to mention the looks I was getting each time I bid clubs.

But on to the play. The jack of hearts was covered by the queen, king and ace. At this point my partner started to shake his head in disbelief as he looked at those clubs. I pur-posely spread them out an extra bit so they would reach all across the table because I was upset that I wasn't the declar-er. My partner counted and recounted my clubs as West began to smolder. He finally played the ace of spades and ruffed a spade and cashed one club discarding a heart. He then recounted the clubs and finally played a second high club discarding a spade. Once again he paused to recount the clubs! West couldn't take it any longer and screamed, 'You had eight clubs in the dummy originally, you have played them twice, I have one left and my partner doesn't have any.'

At this point there are many variations in the play and

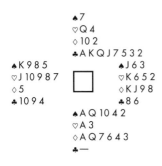

defense. If my partner plays a third club and East ruffs, my partner can overruff and play the ♠Q, smothering the jack and make the hand. However, if East discards the ♠J instead of ruffing, the hand cannot be made. Suffice it to say that my partner went down one even though East did not discard a spade on the third club.

The crowning blow came as we were leaving the table and I heard my partner mutter, 'Eight solid clubs and he leaves me to play the hand in diamonds.'

Life or death

Why do some people excel at this game while others, perhaps more intelligent, struggle so? This question has been asked many times and one hears many different answers. My feeling is that the game has an internal logic that not everyone embraces and it is not a matter of intelligence. After a certain length of time, either you 'get it' or you don't. On the upcoming deal, West was one of those players who 'got it'.

E-W vul.

North
♠ Q 9 4
♡ Q 6 5 3
◊ Q J 5
♣ 8 7 6

West
♠ K J 8 7
♡ J 9
◊ A K 9 4
♣ K Q 5

East
♠ 10 6 3 2
♡ 4 2
◊ 8 3
♣ J 10 9 3 2

South
♠ A 5
♡ A K 10 8 7
◊ 10 7 6 2
♣ A 4

West	North	East	South
			1♡
dbl	2♡	pass	pass
dbl	pass	2♠	3♡
all pass			

Opening lead: ◇A

West's second double was for takeout, showing extras — usually 16 HCP minimum.

East properly responded in a four-card major at the two-level rather than a five-card minor at the three-level. West is supposed to have spades when he makes a takeout double of hearts.

West started smartly with three rounds of diamonds, East ruffing. East exited with the ♣J, which went to declarer's ace. Here, right now, is where it is important that West 'get it'. He must be sharp enough to foresee what is coming. West knows that South has the ◇10 and can use it to discard a club from dummy, 'evening out' that suit for a possible strip and endplay. West also knows that South has the ace of spades from the bidding. If East had four spades to the ace along with five clubs, he would have bid 2♠ over 2♡. So what does it all mean?

It means that if West plays a low club under the ace, declarer will draw trump, discard a club from dummy on the ◇10, and exit a club, which West must win. Now West has to lead away from the ♠K. Death! However, if West has unblocked his ♣K under the ace, he can allow East to win the club exit and return a spade. Life! That's the difference.

The Threepenny Opera

The following deal created such a stir when it was played at the Savoy Bridge Club in Los Angeles that I felt compelled to write it up. The title was a natural because the players were playing for three cents a point.

The cast of characters:

West: George Zahler. Successful builder, tends to be involved in storybook hands.

North: Fran Tsacnaris. House player. Good player.

East: Art Fletcher. Good player who has struck it rich in the pizza parlor business.

South: Doc Freed, plastic surgeon; also a good player who has been known to mold something out of nothing — and vice versa!

Both vul.

North
- ♠ Q J 8 7
- ♡ A 2
- ◊ 6 5
- ♣ A Q 8 5 4

West
- ♠ A K 9 5
- ♡ —
- ◊ Q J 10 7 3
- ♣ K 9 7 6

East
- ♠ 2
- ♡ K Q 9 8 4 3
- ◊ K 9
- ♣ J 10 3 2

South
- ♠ 10 6 4 3
- ♡ J 10 7 6 5
- ◊ A 8 4 2
- ♣ —

West	North	East	South
1◊	pass	1♡	2♣[1]
dbl	pass	pass	2♠
dbl	all pass		

1. Trying to mold something out of nothing.

Opening lead: ◊Q

Doc was up to his old tricks and even though Zahler's doubles rocked the room, Francine in the North seat wasn't exactly unhappy about the goings on. In fact, she was overjoyed.

When the dummy came down, Fletcher in the East seat had several thoughts: (1) It looked for all the world that Doc and Francine, who had exchanged hands, had forgotten to return their original hands to each other; (2) If this was the real dummy he started to estimate his losses in terms of pizza parlors!

Zahler, on the other hand, was in a state of complete shock and for the life of him could not conceive of what was going on. After being allowed to win the first trick with the ◇Q, he finally decided that Fletcher must be void in clubs!

He was right about the void, just had the wrong player. When Zahler shifted to a club, Doc inserted the queen and then played the ace discarding hearts. This was followed with a club ruff, the ◇A and a diamond ruff, club ruff, diamond ruff. At this point Doc had taken seven tricks and these were the remaining cards:

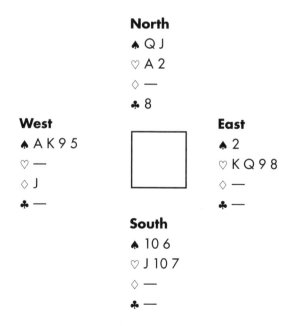

North
♠ Q J
♡ A 2
◇ —
♣ 8

West
♠ A K 9 5
♡ —
◇ J
♣ —

East
♠ 2
♡ K Q 9 8
◇ —
♣ —

South
♠ 10 6
♡ J 10 7
◇ —
♣ —

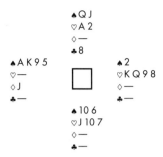

At this point all Doc had to do was ruff a club with the ♠10. West can overruff, but dummy's ♠QJ will take another trick. But in the heat of battle, Doc got greedy and tried to cash the ♡A. The end. Zahler ruffed, drew trumps and took the rest of the tricks for down one. What a deal!

Spot the mistake

Do you fancy yourself a good detective? Let's see. You will be shown how a 3NT contract was played (actually misplayed) and it will be up to you to spot the error(s). If you don't spot it, I hate to say this, but you might have played the hand in the same way!

Neither vul.

North
- ♠ A
- ♡ K 7 5
- ◇ A 4 3
- ♣ K Q 8 6 4 2

West
- ♠ 10 9 7 5 2
- ♡ J 3
- ◇ J 8 7 6
- ♣ 10 7

East
- ♠ K 4 3
- ♡ A 10 6 2
- ◇ 10 9 5
- ♣ A J 9

South
- ♠ Q J 8 6
- ♡ Q 9 8 4
- ◇ K Q 2
- ♣ 5 3

West	North	East	South
	1♣	pass	1♡
pass	3♣	pass	3NT
all pass			

Opening lead: ♠10

Declarer won the opening lead in dummy (nice play), crossed to a diamond honor and led a club to the king, which held. Declarer returned to his hand via a second diamond honor and led a second club to the queen and ace. East exited a diamond to dummy's now blank ace and declarer persisted by leading a third club to East's jack, setting up the suit, as he discarded a heart from his hand. East exited with the king and a spade. South cashed his two spade winners, coming down to the Q-9-8 of hearts; dummy had a good club and the ♡K-x. No good. When a low heart was led to the king, East won the ace and returned a heart to declarer's queen. East's ♡10 took the last trick, capturing South's heart nine.

Okay, you have the facts. What is your verdict?

Declarer strayed when he led a club to the king. This allowed East to duck and shut out the club suit when the ♡K did not prove to be a dummy entry; South took only one club trick. The proper play is a *low* club from dummy at Trick 2. No, this is not a misprint. Leading a low club saves a dummy entry. The best the defense can do is win and shift to a diamond. Declarer wins in the closed hand and leads a second club to the king and ace. The rest is easy because the clubs are established and the ◇A is the entry to get to them.

If you missed this, at least you should take something away with you — the play of the club suit. When you can afford to lose two tricks in the suit and you only have one sure outside dummy entry, play low from both hands the first time around.

One to Remember

It is doubtful whether you have ever seen a deal like this before or will ever see one like it again.

E-W vul.

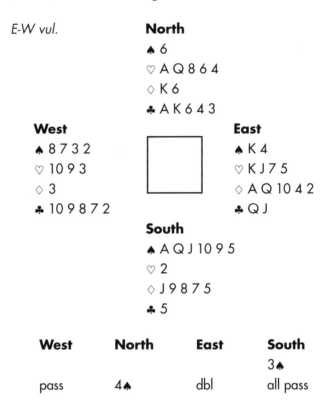

North
- ♠ 6
- ♡ A Q 8 6 4
- ◇ K 6
- ♣ A K 6 4 3

West
- ♠ 8 7 3 2
- ♡ 10 9 3
- ◇ 3
- ♣ 10 9 8 7 2

East
- ♠ K 4
- ♡ K J 7 5
- ◇ A Q 10 4 2
- ♣ Q J

South
- ♠ A Q J 10 9 5
- ♡ 2
- ◇ J 9 8 7 5
- ♣ 5

West	North	East	South
			3♠
pass	4♠	dbl	all pass

Opening lead: ◇ 3

East was afraid he was being talked out of something by his non-vulnerable opponents and rather than appear a coward, he made a somewhat marginal double.

Things started well for East-West. West led his singleton diamond, East grabbed the A-Q and led a low diamond at Trick 3. South stuck in the nine and West ruffed with the ♠7, which dummy could not beat, but the East-West fun was over. After West returned a heart, South grabbed the ace, took the spade finesse and when the king dropped under the ace, he had the rest. After drawing trumps he could discard his losing diamond on a club.

So why is this hand so sensational? Go back to Trick 3. Let's say instead of ruffing the diamond with the seven, West ruffs low and dummy overruffs. Now East has to get in with the ♠K, and he can give West a diamond ruff. So in order to defeat the hand, West has to restrain himself from beating dummy's spade, and must trump low instead?

Not so fast. Ruffing low doesn't beat the hand either. If West ruffs the third diamond low, South lets West take the trick! South does not overruff! Has South gone mad? Not at all. South has the last laugh. After West wins Trick 3, South has no trouble taking the last ten tricks via a spade finesse: six spades, two clubs, the ♡A and the ◇J.

Well, have you ever seen a hand like this before?

The literature of the game is replete with famous deals played by famous players. Here's one played by Harry Fishbein, famous as much for the many different colored berets he sported at tournaments as for his expert play. Let's see if you can match Harry's play on this one. Be sure to cover up the East-West hands.

One for the book

East-West vul.

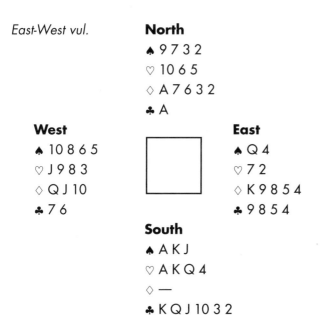

North
♠ 9 7 3 2
♡ 10 6 5
◇ A 7 6 3 2
♣ A

West
♠ 10 8 6 5
♡ J 9 8 3
◇ Q J 10
♣ 7 6

East
♠ Q 4
♡ 7 2
◇ K 9 8 5 4
♣ 9 8 5 4

South
♠ A K J
♡ A K Q 4
◇ —
♣ K Q J 10 3 2

No bidding is given but Harry wound up in 7♣ and the opening lead was the ◇Q. How would you play?

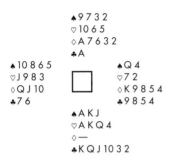

♠9 7 3 2
♡10 6 5
◇A 7 6 3 2
♣A

♠10 8 6 5   ♠Q 4
♡J 9 8 3   ♡7 2
◇Q J 10   ◇K 9 8 5 4
♣7 6   ♣9 8 5 4

♠A K J
♡A K Q 4
◇—
♣K Q J 10 3 2

The problem was that Fishy didn't know what to discard on the ◇A. If hearts were 3-3 or the jack was doubleton, he should discard a spade. However, if the queen of spades was singleton or doubleton, he should discard a heart.

Harry solved the problem by ruffing the opening lead and playing the ♡A, looking for the jack. No luck. His next play was the ♠A looking for the queen. Still no luck. Next the ♡K. Still no jack. Now the ♠K! Success. Finally the ♠Q fell from East. Knowing his ♠J was a winner, Fishy crossed to the ♣A and discarded a heart on the ◇A, ruffed a diamond back to his hand, drew trumps and made the grand.

Had the ♠Q not appeared, Fishbein would have crossed to the ♣A and discarded the ♠J on the ◇A, hoping hearts were 3-3. One for the archives.

An exercise in trump control

This hand brings out two wonderful teaching points, one in declarer play, the other on defense. They deal with handling the play and defense of a two-suited hand.

Both vul.

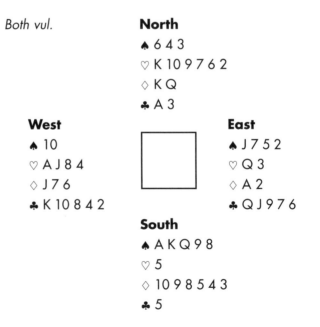

North
♠ 6 4 3
♡ K 10 9 7 6 2
◇ K Q
♣ A 3

West
♠ 10
♡ A J 8 4
◇ J 7 6
♣ K 10 8 4 2

East
♠ J 7 5 2
♡ Q 3
◇ A 2
♣ Q J 9 7 6

South
♠ A K Q 9 8
♡ 5
◇ 10 9 8 5 4 3
♣ 5

West	North	East	South
	1♡	pass	2◇
pass	2♡	pass	2♠
pass	2NT	pass	3♠
pass	4♠	all pass	

Opening lead: ♣4

Everybody at the table knew, or should have known, that South started with six diamonds and five spades. Furthermore, the best defense against two-suiters is to try to force the long hand to trump. If declarer can be forced several times, he may lose control of the hand. This is particularly true when one defender has four trumps. And what counter does the declarer have? If the side suit is not solid, declarer should start playing it at once, perhaps sooner. Nobody will ever be able to calculate the number of contracts thrown out the window because the side suit wasn't attacked soon enough. Nobody.

First, the play as it happened, then the play as it should have happened.

Declarer won the opening lead in dummy, entered the closed hand with a trump, and led a diamond to the king and ace. East returned a club which was ruffed.

At this point both East and South have three trumps. Declarer crossed to the queen of diamonds, returned to his hand with a trump and ruffed a diamond in dummy. East, with J-x of trumps, overruffed dummy and forced declarer with another club. But declarer was in charge. He ruffed, drew East's last trump with his own last trump, ran the diamonds and conceded a heart to make his game.

Had East *not* overruffed the third diamond, South would have no way back to his hand without opening himself up to yet another force, the second force. With this force, South loses control of the hand because now East has more trumps than South. The defensive point is to be wary of overruffing dummy when holding the same trump length

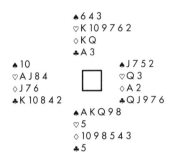

♠ 6 4 3
♡ K 10 9 7 6 2
◊ K Q
♣ A 3

♠ 10
♡ A J 8 4
◊ J 7 6
♣ K 10 8 4 2

♠ J 7 5 2
♡ Q 3
◊ A 2
♣ Q J 9 7 6

♠ A K Q 9 8
♡ 5
◊ 10 9 8 5 4 3
♣ 5

as declarer — if declarer cannot get back to his hand without subjecting himself to a force. The trump trick will come back with dividends — declarer won't be able to use his established side suit.

And what about declarer? Did he do anything wrong? Yes. He erred at Trick 2 when he led a trump to his hand rather than a diamond from dummy. Start the long suit before drawing trumps! Because he didn't, he would have been in serious trouble if East had not overruffed the third diamond. However, if South plays diamonds before spades, he will prevail whether East overruffs or not. Lay it out.

Go with the odds

Conventionally, a double of a final notrump contract, with the doubler's side never having bid, calls for a lead in dummy's first bid suit. Of course after you get the lead you wanted and win the first trick, you have to know what to do next! Cover up the West and South hands and pretend you are East. The hand comes from a U.S Team Trials. To put you at ease, you can't do worse than the expert in the East seat.

North

♠ A Q 10 4 3
♡ K 10 8 5
◊ Q 7
♣ K 4

West

♠ 8 2
♡ J 9 6
◊ 9 6 5 4
♣ A J 10 6

East (you)

♠ K 9 7 6 5
♡ 7 4 2
◊ 10 3
♣ 8 5 3

South

♠ J
♡ A Q 3
◊ A K J 8 2
♣ Q 9 7 2

West	North	East	South
	1♠	pass	2◇ [1]
pass	2♡	pass	2NT
pass	3NT	pass	4NT [2]
pass	6NT	dbl	all pass

1. Game force
2. 17-18 HCP (not forcing and not Blackwood)

Well, you finally got your two cents worth in. Partner obe-diently leads the ♠8, declarer plays low from dummy and you grab the king, felling declarer's jack. What would you lead now? After you decide, take a look at the hidden hands.

The expert who held the East cards shifted to a heart. End of hand, end of story. Declarer was able to take nine tricks in the red suits along with three spades. How should East know to shift to a club rather than a heart? East has to reason like this: If declarer has the ace of hearts along with the jack or queen, and my partner has the ace of clubs, there is a good chance the ace of clubs will go up in flames just as it did. However, if South has the ace of clubs and partner the ace of hearts, South will need four club tricks (he will have to hold AQJx or AQ109) in order for the defense to lose the ace of hearts.

If declarer's clubs are just a touch weaker (AQ10x), the club shift won't cost. East should go with the odds and shift to a club.

When the editors of two rival bridge magazines cross swords in an important tournament, you might expect some fireworks — and you would be right.

Neither vul.

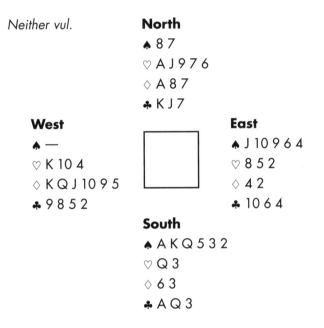

North
- ♠ 8 7
- ♡ A J 9 7 6
- ◇ A 8 7
- ♣ K J 7

West
- ♠ —
- ♡ K 10 4
- ◇ K Q J 10 9 5
- ♣ 9 8 5 2

East
- ♠ J 10 9 6 4
- ♡ 8 5 2
- ◇ 4 2
- ♣ 10 6 4

South
- ♠ A K Q 5 3 2
- ♡ Q 3
- ◇ 6 3
- ♣ A Q 3

West	North	East	South
			1♠
2◇	2♡	pass	3♠
pass	4♠	pass	5♣
pass	6♠	all pass	

Opening lead: ◇K

South was Jean-Paul Meyer, then editor of *Le Bridgeur*, and East, Pierre Schemeil, editor of *Bridge de France* (now defunct). The venue was the Trials to determine the French team for the World Championships.

Meyer won the opening lead in dummy and led a spade. His plan was to draw trumps and take the heart finesse for the contract. Schemeil would have done well to duck the trump, but he feared South might have no outside losers and would let the eight run as a safety play. He covered.

Meyer won the trick and even though he had two spade losers, he had chances. He led the ♡Q, which was covered and taken by the ace, and a second trump from dummy was covered and taken by declarer. A heart went to the nine and the jack of hearts provided a parking place for declarer's losing diamond. It still wasn't over.

A diamond was ruffed in the closed hand and three rounds of clubs followed, the lead ending in dummy. This was the three-card end position, North to play:

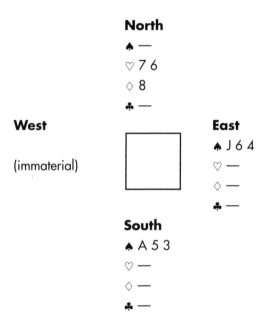

North
♠ —
♡ 7 6
♢ 8
♣ —

West

(immaterial)

East
♠ J 6 4
♡ —
♢ —
♣ —

South
♠ A 5 3
♡ —
♢ —
♣ —

A diamond was led from dummy and East ruffed with the six. Meyer underruffed with the three and when East exited with the four, South took the last two tricks with the five and the ace.

Bien joué, Jean-Paul.

A forlorn hope

When partner puts you in a grand slam, the first move most of us make when the dummy hits is to make sure we have all the aces — or at least a void in a suit missing the ace. The next check is the trump suit. It's easier on the central nervous system when the trump suit is solid in a grand slam. Having said that, how would you like to be playing a grand slam with the singleton king of trumps in dummy facing the AJ9843 in your hand? Well, excluding a major miracle like the Q10 doubleton, is there any hope?

Neither vul.

North
♠ A K J 3 2
♡ K
♢ A Q 4
♣ A J 9 3

West
♠ 9 7 5
♡ Q 2
♢ J 10 9 8 3
♣ 10 7 6

East
♠ Q 10 8
♡ 10 7 6 5
♢ 7 6
♣ Q 8 4 2

South
♠ 6 4
♡ A J 9 8 4 3
♢ K 5 2
♣ K 5

West	North	East	South
			1♡
pass	2♠	pass	3♡
pass	4♣	pass	4♡
pass	4NT	pass	5♡
pass	5NT	pass	6♡
pass	7♡	all pass	

Opening lead: ◊J

The modern trend is *not* to make a strong jump shift with a two-suited hand. Jump shifts should be made with one of three types of hands: (1) a one-suited hand; (2) a hand with strong support for partner's suit; (3) a balanced hand with five-card suit and 17-18 HCP that bids notrump next. The North hand didn't fit any of those categories and should have responded 1♠.

Also, it would have helped if North-South had been playing Keycard Blackwood, where the queen of the agreed suit can be shown or denied in the Blackwood response.

North couldn't believe that South didn't own the ♡Q having rebid the suit three times. (The third heart rebid was a mistake. South is better advised to bid 4♠ rather than mention a broken suit three times facing a jump shift.)

The opening lead was won in dummy with the queen and the ♡K cashed. South crossed to his hand with a club and played the ♡A, discarding a spade from the table. A miracle occurred: West played the queen. There were still chances. Declarer continued with the ace-king and a spade ruff followed by the ace of clubs and a club ruff. Dummy was entered with the ◇A leading to this three-card ending:

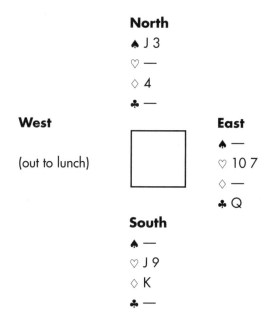

North
♠ J 3
♡ —
◇ 4
♣ —

West

(out to lunch)

East
♠ —
♡ 10 7
◇ —
♣ Q

South
♠ —
♡ J 9
◇ K
♣ —

```
        ♠ J
        ♡ —
        ◇ 4
        ♣ J
(out to lunch)  ┌──┐   ♠ —
               │  │   ♡ 10 7
               └──┘   ◇ —
                      ♣ Q
        ♠ —
        ♡ J 9
        ◇ K
        ♣ —
```

The ♠J is played from dummy and East has no answer. If East discards the ♣Q, South discards the ◇K and takes the last two tricks *en passant* with the ♡J-9. If East ruffs, South overruffs, draws the last trump and cashes the ◇K. East has no answer. So who needs Keycard Blackwood? Just kidding.

MVC — Most Valuable Card

Most rubber bridge players complain bitterly that they don't hold as many aces and kings as their opponents. Yet you seldom hear anyone complain about not holding enough deuces! Yet the deuce has proven time and again to be the most valuable card in the deck... in the hands of an expert.

Both vul.

North
♠ 9 4
♡ A Q 9 4
◇ J 9 7 4
♣ Q 9 3

West
♠ 10 8 3 2
♡ J 7 5 3 2
◇ 3
♣ 8 6 5

East
♠ K 7 6
♡ 10 8
◇ A Q 10 8 6 5
♣ 7 4

South
♠ A Q J 5
♡ K 6
◇ K 2
♣ A K J 10 2

West	North	East	South
	pass	2◇[1]	dbl
pass	2NT	pass	3♣
pass	4♣	pass	4NT
pass	5◇	dbl	6♣
all pass			

1. Weak

Opening lead: ◇3

North-South belong in 6NT (with the spade finesse working) because a diamond ruff will immediately defeat 6♣. But South made 6♣ anyway!

South knew from the bidding (and the lead) that West had led a singleton. However, from East's point of view, the lead was either a singleton or from 3-2 doubleton. When East played the ace, South, blessed with the deuce, dropped the king! Who can blame East for thinking that partner had led from the 3-2 doubleton? East shifted to a trump at Trick 2. Suddenly South was alive, alive!

He won the trump shift in dummy with the nine, took a successful spade finesse, returned to dummy with the ♣Q, finessed the spade again, and ruffed a low spade with dummy's last trump. Success was approaching. He reentered the closed hand with the ♡K, drew the last trump and discarded his precious, precious, deuce of diamonds on a heart winner. Slam bid and made.

As an aside, players often ask what is the real difference between money bridge and tournament bridge? Maybe this true story will answer that question.

Many years ago when I was seventeen years old (misspent youth?) playing at the Ardmore Bridge Club in Los Angeles, they had tournament bridge downstairs and rubber bridge or money bridge upstairs. I played in both — I didn't tell them my real age so I could play for real money.

Neither group was particularly fond of the other and when the rubber bridge players walked up the stairs they looked neither left nor right at what they considered a lower form of life, the tournament player. They argued that if these people thought they were so good, why didn't they come upstairs and play for money? The tournament players on the other hand, felt contaminated in the presence of rubber bridge players and would only go upstairs at all because the restrooms were there. They argued that if these rubber bridge players thought they were such hot shots, why didn't they come downstairs and play a game of skill, not one that

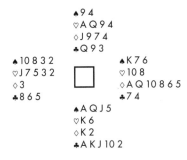

depended only upon who got the most aces and kings.

And so it came to pass that one afternoon after the duplicate game ended there was the usual mass exodus upstairs. Included in this exodus was the reigning queen of duplicate bridge in Los Angeles at that time, Malvine Klausner. Her husband, Sigfried, had invented Kem Cards. When she finally made it to the Ladies room she found a full house so she headed next door to the Men's room! When she emerged, her friends were aghast.

'Malvine, do you know where you were?'

'Yes, I know where I was'.

'Well, was there anybody else in there?'

'Well, there were a few guys in there, but they were only rubber bridge players.'

No problem

One doesn't win thirteen World Championships without being a great, great, player. Benito Garozzo is just that. Here is a hand from a match in Johannesburg, South Africa, with Garozzo sitting South.

Neither vul.

North
♠ —
♡ K 6 5 4 3
◇ K J 10 8 6
♣ K 8 6

West
♠ Q 9 4 3 2
♡ Q J 10 8
◇ 9 7 5 3
♣ —

East
♠ A K J 10 5
♡ 7
◇ Q 4
♣ 10 9 5 4 2

South
♠ 8 7 6
♡ A 9 2
◇ A 2
♣ A Q J 7 3

West	North	East	South
	1♡	1♠	2♣
3♠	4♣	pass	4◊
4♠	pass	pass	5♡
pass	5♠	pass	6♣
all pass			

Opening lead: ♠3

West should have leaped to 4♠ earlier, but the contract might have been the same regardless. In the other room, Garozzo's teammates played in 5♠ doubled down one for a loss of 100 points. When dummy was tabled, the commentators could see the foul breaks in both clubs and hearts, not to mention the missing ◊Q, and all thought that even the great Garozzo had bitten off more than he could chew. Hah!

He ruffed the opening lead in dummy and, suspecting foul distribution, ran the ◊J at Trick 2. When that held he crossed to the ◊A, returned to dummy with the ♣K (no noticeable flinch when West showed out) and began to play high diamonds through East. There was no way out for East.

He and Garozzo each discarded hearts on the third diamond, but East ruffed the fourth diamond with the ♣9 which Garozzo overruffed. Garozzo ruffed a spade in dummy and played a fifth diamond. If East ruffs, he loses his trump trick, declarer losing a spade in the end. If East refuses to ruff, Garozzo discards a spade and plays winning hearts, losing a only trump trick in the end.

Molto bene, Benito.

A technical difficulty

Many years ago, teaching a morning class, I met Rea. She must have liked the class, because after the second class she presented me with a bag lunch. She also invited my parents and me to her home to meet her husband, etc. Soon we were all good friends. After my mother passed away, she was very nice to my father. Are you getting the picture? Rea was a beautiful person. She also had a great passion for bridge and had been playing her whole life; she was about sixty years old when I met her. Eventually she asked if she could kibitz me in a tournament. No problem. Then she wanted to hire me as a professional partner. I was a little reluctant, fearing I might involuntarily react to a bad play or say something I would regret. Finally I agreed. We decided to play in a two-session event in Coronado.

We met an hour before game time at our designated table. Rea came to the table armed with lunches for both of us (of course), the *New York Times*, the *Los Angeles Times*, the *San Diego Tribune* and the *Wall Street Journal*. She also brought with her every convention card she had ever used in her life. And let's not forget the box of long Turkish cigarettes (in those days, you could still smoke at the table).

I told Rea we would play a simple system and we would have *fun*. She said she was sure we would have fun as long as the director did not come over to our table — that was the only thing that really bothered her. I assured her he wouldn't. This is what happened:

1st round: Rea revokes (director called)
2nd round: Rea leads out of turn (director called)
3rd round: Rea drops some cards on the floor
             (director called)
4th round: Rea bids out of turn (director called)

I might add that on the boards where the director came over to the table, as a result of the penalties assessed against us, we wound up with four zeros. On the other four boards, the opponents were playing like geniuses, not to mention Rea's underruff with the setting trick on one of them. The bottom line was that after eight boards we had eight zeros! Worse, I had put my name first on the entry blank so when the scores came out everyone would see that we had the lowest score in the history of tournament bridge and my name would stand out like a beacon.

This is what happened on the first board of the fifth round. Keep in mind Rea is a little off balance because of the director being called over so often, and I wasn't exactly at my steadiest either.

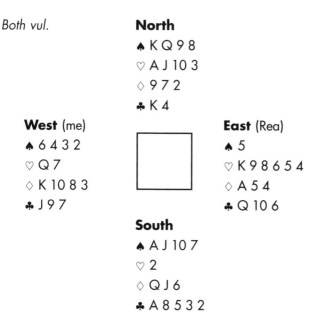

Both vul.

North
♠ K Q 9 8
♡ A J 10 3
◇ 9 7 2
♣ K 4

West (me)
♠ 6 4 3 2
♡ Q 7
◇ K 10 8 3
♣ J 9 7

East (Rea)
♠ 5
♡ K 9 8 6 5 4
◇ A 5 4
♣ Q 10 6

South
♠ A J 10 7
♡ 2
◇ Q J 6
♣ A 8 5 3 2

West	North	East	South
			1♣
pass	1♡	pass	1♠
pass	4♠	all pass	

Opening lead: ◇ 3

We had survived the bidding and opening lead with no director call. Maybe our luck would change. Rea won the ace of diamonds, returned a diamond to my king and declarer won the third round of the suit. Rea and I had

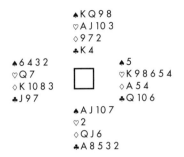

♠KQ98
♡AJ103
◇972
♣K4

♠6432　　　　♠5
♡Q7　　　　　♡K98654
◇K1083　　　◇A54
♣J97　　　　　♣Q106

♠AJ107
♡2
◇QJ6
♣A8532

actually taken two tricks without anything happening.

From here declarer has a high crossruff for the rest of the tricks, but instead he opted to play two rounds of trumps ending in his hand, Rea discarding the ♡9 on the second spade.

Next, declarer led a heart to the ace and then a low heart intending to ruff. Rea went up with her king, squashed my queen, and now the J-10 of hearts in dummy were high. I knew it had been too good to be true.

At this point, declarer began to reflect upon his good fortune as Rea put down her cards to light up one of her long Turkish cigarettes. However, when she picked up her cards, she didn't pick up the unplayed cards, she picked up the ones she had already played. In other words, she now had a trump, the ◇A, and best of all the ♡K!

Declarer, who had blocked the trump suit, cashed the ♠A, Rea following, and me not noticing (I was gone by this time). He then crossed to the ♣K, drew my last trump and played the good (he thought) heart jack. Not so fast. Rea was right there with the king! People can set up suits against Rea and me, but they can't use them! *Director*!

Strangely, the director was right next to our table. He had learned where to stand. It was a bit difficult to explain what had happened, but after he heard, his ruling was 'that the play had gotten out of hand' (no kidding) and awarded them average plus. Rea and I high-fived each other. Average minus seemed like a top to us. They appealed. They won the appeal. Another zero.

You may not believe this, but Rea and I finished above average in this event.

Everyone is familiar with using Stayman over a 1NT or 2NT opening to locate a 4-4 major suit fit. But what about locating a 4-4 minor suit fit? More often than not a 4-4 fit plays one or two tricks better than notrump.

Minor-suit Stayman

Neither vul.

North
♠ K 5 4
♡ 3 2
◇ A Q J 6
♣ A Q 5 4

West
♠ 10 7
♡ Q J 10 9 8 5
◇ 8
♣ J 9 8 6

East
♠ Q J 9 8
♡ 6 4
◇ 10 9 3 2
♣ 10 7 2

South
♠ A 6 3 2
♡ A K 7
◇ K 7 5 4
♣ K 3

West	North	East	South
			1NT
pass	2♠[1]	pass	3◇
pass	6◇	all pass	

1. Minor Suit Stayman

Opening lead: ♡Q

North-South were playing transfer responses to show the majors; 2◇ was a transfer to hearts and 2♡ a transfer to spades. This method frees up the 2♠ response to show something else. Many use it as Minor Suit Stayman. Opener rebids 2NT without a minor and bids a minor with four- or five-card length. In this case a 4-4 diamond fit was uncovered and North wisely opted to play the 4-4. Notice

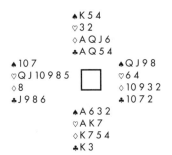

♠K 5 4
♡3 2
◇A Q J 6
♣A Q 5 4

♠10 7
♡Q J 10 9 8 5
◇8
♣J 9 8 6

♠Q J 9 8
♡6 4
◇10 9 3 2
♣10 7 2

♠A 6 3 2
♡A K 7
◇K 7 5 4
♣K 3

that North-South have 33 HCP between the two hands but there are only eleven tricks in notrump. In diamonds, if played carefully, a ruff in one hand or the other produces a twelfth trick.

South won the opening lead and cashed the A-Q of diamonds. Had diamonds divided 3-2, South would draw the last trump and ruff a heart in dummy or a club in his hand for the twelfth trick. When East showed up with four diamonds, it was too dangerous (and silly) to try to ruff a heart in dummy. It must be safer to ruff a club in the closed hand. South cashed the king-ace of clubs and ruffed a low club with a low trump. The ◇K was cashed, dummy entered with a spade and the last trump drawn. Declarer had garnered twelve tricks via: five diamond tricks including the club ruff (one more diamond trick than could be taken at notrump), three clubs, two spades and two hearts.

When slam is in the air, it pays to know how to uncover a 4-4 minor-suit fit as well as a 4-4 major-suit fit. Minor suits shouldn't be treated like orphans. With a 4-4 fit, 31 HCP between the two hands is usually enough — unless the trump suit has two losers, or the opponents have two aces or a cashing A-K in the same suit. Any of these will derail your train before it leaves the station.

One of the first rules you give a beginner in defensive play is to play 'third hand high' when partner leads a low card and dummy has small cards. However, no rule in bridge is without exception; you just have to know when to invoke the exception. This hand will point you in the right direction.

The exception proves the rule

E-W vul.

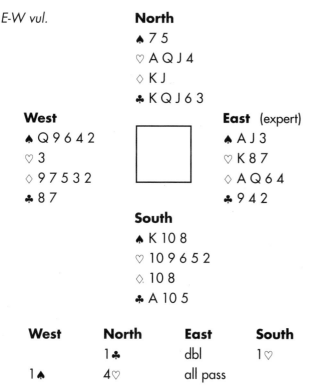

North
♠ 7 5
♡ A Q J 4
◇ K J
♣ K Q J 6 3

West
♠ Q 9 6 4 2
♡ 3
◇ 9 7 5 3 2
♣ 8 7

East (expert)
♠ A J 3
♡ K 8 7
◇ A Q 6 4
♣ 9 4 2

South
♠ K 10 8
♡ 10 9 6 5 2
◇ 10 8
♣ A 10 5

West	North	East	South
	1♣	dbl	1♡
1♠	4♡	all pass	

Opening lead: ♠4

At a different vulnerability West might have considered a 4♠ sacrifice. Just as well he didn't here, because 4♡ can be defeated — with good defense.

Consider the hand from East's point of view. East is looking at three sure tricks in his own hand and if partner has the ♠K the hand can be defeated two tricks with two spades, two diamonds and a heart. However if partner has the ♠Q (the lead of a low card suggests a high honor), it is going to be difficult to get partner in before those clubs

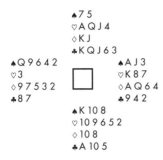

♠ 7 5
♡ A Q J 4
◇ K J
♣ K Q J 6 3

♠ Q 9 6 4 2   ♠ A J 3
♡ 3   ♡ K 8 7
◇ 9 7 5 3 2   ◇ A Q 6 4
♣ 8 7   ♣ 9 4 2

♠ K 10 8
♡ 10 9 6 5 2
◇ 10 8
♣ A 10 5

come showering down, as declarer pitches diamonds.

In order to ensure a later entry to partner's hand, and perhaps give up an extra undertrick, East plays the ♠J at Trick 1. South wins the king and takes a losing heart finesse. Now East leads a low spade over to that presumed queen and the diamond through defeats the contract one trick. The defenders collect two diamonds, a spade and a heart. Well done, East.

P.S. This is a scary hand to write about because it is a major league exception. If you try this play and it doesn't work, don't write, don't call, and don't email. I don't know you.

Experience shows

It's not every partner who will trust you enough to table an eight-card side suit headed by 100 honors! If you have one of these partners, you had better know how to handle the play of a sticky 4-4 trump fit.

Both vul.

North
♠ K J 8 5
♡ 2
◇ A Q J 10 7 6 5 4
♣ —

West
♠ 6
♡ K Q 10 8 4 3
◇ 9 8
♣ A J 3 2

East
♠ 10 4 3 2
♡ A J 7
◇ K 3
♣ K Q 7 6

South
♠ A Q 9 7
♡ 9 6 5
◇ 2
♣ 10 9 8 5 4

West	North	East	South
	1◇	dbl	1♠
4♡	4♠	pass	pass
5♡	5♠	dbl	all pass

Opening lead: ♡K

After everyone had digested this unbelievable dummy, West continued with a second heart. It is almost always best defense to force the hand with the long side suit to trump. The heart continuation was ruffed in dummy and declarer continued with the A-Q of diamonds, trumping East's king as the suit split a friendly 2-2.

At this point both North and South each have three trumps and East has four. Trouble! An inexperienced player might get excited and play the ace and another spade to dummy's jack. The inexperienced player will take exactly two more tricks. Assuming a diamond is led from dummy, East trumps and the most South can do is take each of his trumps separately. Down an ignominious four.

A more experienced player will cross to the ♠J and play a high diamond intending to discard if East doesn't ruff. Say East ruffs. South overtrumps with the ace and leads the queen of spades to dummy's king setting up East's ten of spades. No matter. Dummy still has the ♠8 and when winning diamonds are continued, the most East can score is that ♠10. Making five.

South's line of play works even when West has a second spade. West trumps the third round of diamonds and plays a club forcing dummy to ruff. Dummy now has the blank ♠K, South the A-Q and East the 10-4. Diamonds are continued. When East trumps, South overtrumps with the ace, enters dummy with the ♠K and takes the balance.

It helps to have experience playing hands like this, to say the least.

Have you ever wondered what it would feel like to make the world's greatest bid? Erik Paulsen, a former World Champion, once had that feeling playing in the Blue Ribbon Pairs; this is the hand that inspired it.

It takes a genius

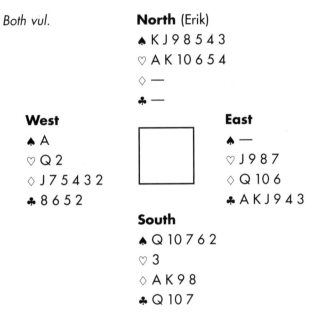

Both vul.

North (Erik)
- ♠ K J 9 8 5 4 3
- ♡ A K 10 6 5 4
- ◇ —
- ♣ —

West
- ♠ A
- ♡ Q 2
- ◇ J 7 5 4 3 2
- ♣ 8 6 5 2

East
- ♠ —
- ♡ J 9 8 7
- ◇ Q 10 6
- ♣ A K J 9 4 3

South
- ♠ Q 10 7 6 2
- ♡ 3
- ◇ A K 9 8
- ♣ Q 10 7

West	North	East	South
		1♣	1♠
2♣	5NT	pass	6♠
dbl	7♠	pass	pass
dbl	redbl	all pass	

Opening lead: ♠A (before it gets away)

This bidding diagram requires a 'little' explanation, as do all genius-inspired bids. Paulsen's leap to 5NT was the Grand Slam Force, asking South to describe his spade holding. In their methods the response of 6♠ showed the ace or king but denied the queen. With two of the top three honors, responder was supposed to leap to a grand. In addition, a 6♣ response denied the ace or king.

When Paulsen heard the 6♠ bid, he 'knew' seven spades

was cold. As this was tournament bridge he had some calculating to do. Assuming 7♠ is cold, North-South are entitled to a score of 2210. Passing 6♠ doubled, making seven, is 'only' 1860 points. Clearly it can't be right to pass 6♠. What about redoubling? Paulsen calculated that 6♠ redoubled with an overtrick would bring in 2420, more than seven spades making seven.

So why didn't Paulsen redouble? Because he is a genius. He realized that at the other tables seven spades would be doubled. Seven spades doubled making seven, vulnerable, is 2470 points — more than six spades redoubled making seven! What else could he do? He couldn't settle for a mere 2420 points when everybody(!) else would be garnering 2470 points! He made the only logical call under the circumstances. And for kickers, just to make sure he got his top, he redoubled. If you don't agree with Erik's action on this deal, you might speak to him about it... at a distance.

My favorite Erik Paulsen story is when he returned to Downey, California after winning the World Championship and went back to his roots at his favorite local club. Nobody had believed he would ever show up there again. During the course of the game, Erik and his partner were competing in spades against two fellows who were bidding hearts. When the opponents arrived in three hearts, Erik thought they could probably make it and, besides, they wouldn't dare double him in three spades, World Champion and all, so he bid it — loudly, just to make sure he wasn't doubled.

The 3♠ bid was met with a resounding double by his left-hand opponent. Erik turned to his opponent and asked, 'Do you know who I am?'

'Yes, I know who you are.'

'Do you know how many master points I have?'

'No, I don't, but do you know how many spades I have?'

A well-read declarer

Every so often a play comes up that you only read about in books. If it should happen to you, it pays to have read the right books! Cover up the East-West hands and we'll see what you've been reading these days.

E-W vul.

North
♠ J 4
♡ 10 8 3
◇ A J 10 9 8
♣ J 6 4

West
♠ K 9 5
♡ A 9 7 6 5 4 2
◇ —
♣ K Q 7

East
♠ 10 8 7 3
♡ J
◇ K 7 6 5 4 3
♣ 10 2

South
♠ A Q 6 2
♡ K Q
◇ Q 2
♣ A 9 8 5 3

West	North	East	South
1♡	pass	pass	1NT
2♡	3◇	pass	3NT
all pass			

Opening lead: ♡6

You play low from dummy and capture East's jack. At Trick 2 you run the ◇Q which holds, West discarding a low spade. How do you continue?

You are in a bit of trouble. With no dummy entry to the diamonds and all the missing honors marked to your left, it looks bad. But there is a way out. Play a second diamond to the ace and then a third diamond discarding your last heart! What you have done is create a heart stopper in dummy. If the opponents want to play hearts, dummy is going to take a trick in the suit.

In practice East won the ◇K and shifted to a club ducked to West's queen. West didn't have much choice, so he did his best by playing the ace and a heart putting dummy on play. Dummy's two remaining diamonds were cashed and now everyone was down to four cards. Dummy had the J-x of both black suits, West, the K-x of both black suits and South, the A-x of clubs and the A-Q of spades. South played the ace and a club giving up a trick to West's king, but took his eighth and ninth tricks with the A-Q of spades.

So, have you been reading the right books?

How would you like to judge a $20 bridge bet? The hand in question is from a World Championship match, U.S vs. France. I was South, playing with Bob Hamman when the deal came up. We each thought that the other had made such a horrible bid that we bet $20 on who made the worst bid. He was so sure that it was me that he allowed me to give the deal to two mutually acceptable impartial judges. He said that if they both didn't agree with him, I would win the bet. Let's see how you would have decided. Sitting North, you are vulnerable against not, and you gaze at:

You be the judge

♠ A K Q 10 6 5   ♡ A Q 10 4   ◇ 10 4   ♣ 10

The bidding goes:

West	North (Bob)	East	South (Eddie)
		pass	pass
1♣	dbl	3◇	3♠
4♣	4♠	5◇	dbl
pass	?		

The question is whether to leave in my double or to pull it to 5♠. Make up your mind before looking at the full deal.

N-S vul.

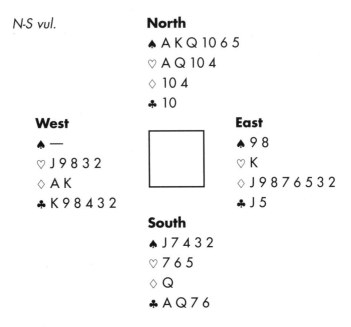

North
♠ A K Q 10 6 5
♡ A Q 10 4
◇ 10 4
♣ 10

West
♠ —
♡ J 9 8 3 2
◇ A K
♣ K 9 8 4 3 2

East
♠ 9 8
♡ K
◇ J 9 8 7 6 5 3 2
♣ J 5

South
♠ J 7 4 3 2
♡ 7 6 5
◇ Q
♣ A Q 7 6

As it happened, Hamman passed and we managed to beat it a trick. I led a heart to Bob's ace and he shifted to the singleton ten of clubs covered by the jack and my ace. When I returned a club, declarer inserted the nine and Bob ruffed, but that was our last trick. After ruffing Bob played a spade which dummy ruffed with the king. The ace of diamonds drew trumps and the ♣K was good for a spade pitch. Plus a measly 100 points.

Of course we make five spades in a breeze, losing one heart (probably) and one diamond. Hamman thought my double was atrocious holding a singleton diamond and an offensive-type hand. I thought that with my weak spades and misplaced ♣Q I did not want to make a forcing pass and invite 5♠. I thought he should have pulled the double.

Have you ever heard of the operation being a success but the patient dying? That's what happened here. I won the bet, but we lost 11 IMPs on the board.

How would you like to receive condolences on a hand you played, everyone telling you that you couldn't logically have made the hand after that lead, only to discover a day later that the hand was cold. Well, it happened to me in a practice match against the Dallas Aces. Misery. See if you can do better; you can't do worse. Cover up the East-West hands.

Neither vul.

North
- ♠ 5 4 3
- ♡ A 10
- ◇ A Q 6 4
- ♣ 10 7 6 5

West
- ♠ K Q 9
- ♡ K 9 7 4 2
- ◇ J 3
- ♣ J 4 3

East
- ♠ 6 2
- ♡ Q J 8 6 5 3
- ◇ 9 8 7 5
- ♣ 2

South
- ♠ A J 10 8 7
- ♡ —
- ◇ K 10 2
- ♣ A K Q 9 8

West	North	East	South
			1♣
pass	1◇	pass	2♠
pass	3♣	pass	3♠
pass	4♡	pass	5♣
pass	6♣	all pass	

Opening lead: ◇J

I happen to believe in opening 1♣ with really strong hands that have 5-5 in the blacks (hands that have jump shift potential). A 1♣ opening makes it easier for partner to respond with a marginal hand. As it happened, we wound up in a great contract — had I made it. How would you play

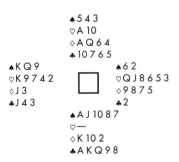

♠ 5 4 3
♡ A 10
◇ A Q 6 4
♣ 10 7 6 5

♠ K Q 9
♡ K 9 7 4 2
◇ J 3
♣ J 4 3

♠ 6 2
♡ Q J 8 6 5 3
◇ 9 8 7 5
♣ 2

♠ A J 10 8 7
♡ —
◇ K 10 2
♣ A K Q 9 8

it? West started with J-x-x of trumps, East had a singleton.

I should have won the opening lead in dummy with the queen, played the ♡A, discarding a spade, and ruffed a heart stripping that suit. Next I play the AKQ of clubs followed by overtaking the ◇K with dummy's ace leaving the ◇10 as a return entry to my hand.

With West stripped of safe red suit exits, the stage is set to lead a spade to the jack. As it happens West has the K-Q-x of spades, so the best he can do is win and exit a heart, a ruff and a sluff. I ruff with my last trump discarding a spade from dummy. It's all over now but the shouting. I play the ace and ruff a spade setting up my spades and use the ◇10 to get back to my hand.

Did you make it?

Four for four

How would you like to see one of the most deceptive hands ever played? After all, how much better can you do than make a deceptive play all four suits?

N-S vul.

North
♠ A Q 9 3
♡ K 8 7 6
◇ K 3
♣ 5 4 2

West
♠ 10 8 2
♡ A 3
◇ A 9 2
♣ Q 8 7 6 3

East
♠ K 7 6 4
♡ 5 2
◇ Q 10 8 7 6 4
♣ 10

South
♠ J 5
♡ Q J 10 9 4
◇ J 5
♣ A K J 9

West	North	East	South
pass	pass	pass	1♡
2♣	4♡[1]	all pass	

1. Must have overlooked his hand the first time around.

Opening lead: ♣6

Knowing that East must have a singleton club, and also knowing that if the ♣J took the first trick, West would also know East had a singleton club (the play of the ten denied the nine), South won the first trick with the ace, implanting in West's mind that East had the jack of clubs. Deceptive play #1 (winning the opening lead with the ace rather than the jack — purposely giving up a sure trick). Ha!

At Trick 2 South led the ♡J, trying to make it appear that he was finessing. The idea was to get West to duck so he wouldn't inadvertently win the ♡A and lead a club over to partner's jack, only to see his partner ruff the trick. West ducked the trick and perforce won the next heart lead. Deceptive play #2 (leading the ♡J).

In with the ♡A, West led a club over to East's jack. Oops, East didn't have the jack, South did and he won the trick with that card. At least somebody had the jack of clubs. South had now got his club trick back and avoided a ruff in the process. Not through with West, South tried the ♢J (knowing full well that West had the ace given the over-call). West ducked again. North won the king. Deceptive play #3 (leading the ♢J).

Now that West had turned up with both red aces and the ♣Q, South knew that East must have the ♠K, or else West would have had 13 HCP and would have opened the bidding. The ace of spades was played from dummy followed by a low spade. East figured that his partner must have the jack or else why didn't declarer take a spade finesse? East ducked and the ♠J took the trick. Deceptive play #4 (the ace and a low spade).

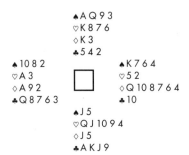

```
        ♠A Q 9 3
        ♡K 8 7 6
        ◇K 3
        ♣5 4 2
♠1 0 8 2          ♠K 7 6 4
♡A 3              ♡5 2
◇A 9 2            ◇Q 10 8 7 6 4
♣Q 8 7 6 3        ♣10
        ♠J 5
        ♡Q J 10 9 4
        ◇J 5
        ♣A K J 9
```

Believe it or not, South wasn't through yet! He crossed to the dummy with a heart and led the ♠Q, covered by the king and ruffed by South. Have you noticed that the ♠9 in dummy is high? Declarer did. He cashed a high club, ruffed a club and discarded his remaining diamond on the ♠9. Making six! Bridge is such an easy game.

Timing again

Do you attack your longest and strongest suit at notrump to drive out the opposing honor(s)? Of course you do — most of the time. But most of the time is not all of the time. And the reason for not doing it might be because you don't have 'time'. The following is a 'timing' example submitted by Pedro Paulo Assumpcao of Brazil as an entry to the BOLS bridge prize competition.

E-W vul.

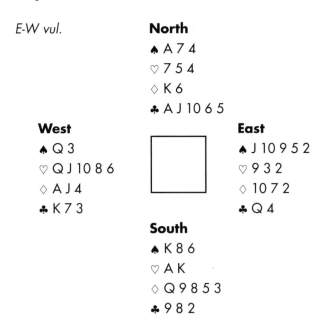

North
♠ A 7 4
♡ 7 5 4
◇ K 6
♣ A J 10 6 5

West
♠ Q 3
♡ Q J 10 8 6
◇ A J 4
♣ K 7 3

East
♠ J 10 9 5 2
♡ 9 3 2
◇ 10 7 2
♣ Q 4

South
♠ K 8 6
♡ A K
◇ Q 9 8 5 3
♣ 9 8 2

West	**North**	**East**	**South**
1♡	2♣	pass	3NT
all pass			

Opening lead: ♡Q

You start with four tricks in the majors and must develop *five* tricks in the minors, but you only have one heart stopper left which means you can only let them in *once*. Scary.

It looks normal to start on clubs, but can you see what will happen? After you lose a club trick and a heart comes back, even though you can run the clubs (via a second finesse) you only have eight tricks: four clubs, two hearts and two spades. Worse, you don't have 'time' to set up your ninth trick in diamonds. When you finally get around to leading a diamond, West will step up with the ace and cash the setting tricks in hearts. What you must do is lead a low *diamond* at Trick 2. Now let's see what West does.

If he ducks, you win the king, cross to the ♠K and run the ♣9, which loses to the queen. Back comes a heart which you win, and now you run the ♣8. When that holds, you have four clubs and nine tricks: four clubs, two hearts, two spades and one diamond.

If West rises with the ◇A at Trick 2 and clears hearts, you are still alive if diamonds break 3-3 or the J-10 is doubleton. In either case you will only need *one* club trick. The bottom line is that you don't have time to start clubs; you must start diamonds.

Stranger than fiction

Bridge is a strange, strange, game. With four minds plotting different strategies, anything can happen. The following is a hand from the Blue Ribbon Pairs at the Fall Nationals in Coronado. Dorothy Hayden (now Dorothy Hayden Truscott) was playing with B.J. Becker. Becker was South.

Both vul.

North
- ♠ 3
- ♡ K 10 7 5 2
- ◇ A Q J 8 6 5
- ♣ Q

West
- ♠ A Q J 7 6
- ♡ 9
- ◇ 10 7 2
- ♣ 8 6 5 4

East
- ♠ K 9 8 2
- ♡ 8 6 4
- ◇ —
- ♣ J 10 9 7 3 2

South
- ♠ 10 5 4
- ♡ A Q J 3
- ◇ K 9 4 3
- ♣ A K

West	North	East	South
			1NT
pass	2◇	pass	2♡
pass	4NT	pass	5♡
pass	6♡	dbl	6NT
all pass			

I think the bidding requires a 'little' explanation. I bet nobody can figure out what 2◇ meant. It was natural! Becker and Hayden were the only pair in the tournament (the country, the planet, the universe?) not playing Stayman or transfers. When Becker bid 2♡, also natural, Dorothy dragged out old trusty Blackwood and set the hand in a comfortable 6♡ contract. Well, comfortable until East doubled to ask for an unusual lead, normally dummy's first bid suit. Becker, realizing that East must be void in diamonds and that 6♡ had no chance, ran to 6NT!

Now the spotlight was on West. Had he decided to lead a spade, the contract would have gone down four! But no, West led a diamond, the suit East wanted against a heart contract, not against a notrump contract! Anyway Becker wrapped up the first thirteen tricks for the coldest top this side of Antarctica.

As an aside, I played in this event with Bob Hamman, who had a bad cold and was running a fever at the time. Becker and Hayden arrived at our table and on the first hand Bob wound up in 4♠ after I had raised his spades. Becker made his opening lead, and as I was putting down the dummy, Hamman suddenly threw up! Not a second later Becker said, 'It wasn't *that* bad of a dummy, Bob.'

Working without a net

Here's an example of what I went through when I played with my favorite (at one time I could have put 'only') partner, Billy Eisenberg. Supposedly we had methods to cover most contingencies, including 'interrupted Blackwood'. If our opponents had the nerve to interfere with our Blackwood responses, we played something called Keycard DOPI. Even though you couldn't care less about this method, I am going to tell it to you anyway.

If they interfered over our 4NT bid, we doubled with zero or three keycards. We passed with one or four keycards and bid the next step up with two keycards. Wait, it's not over yet. We skipped a step when we had two keycards plus the queen of trumps. Got it? Good. Now follow the action. I'm North and Billy is South.

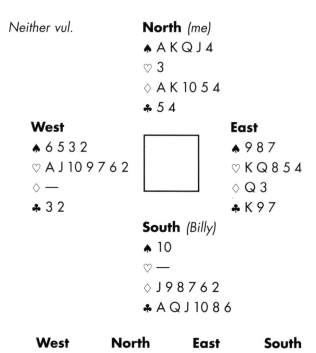

Neither vul.

North *(me)*
♠ A K Q J 4
♡ 3
◇ A K 10 5 4
♣ 5 4

West
♠ 6 5 3 2
♡ A J 10 9 7 6 2
◇ —
♣ 3 2

East
♠ 9 8 7
♡ K Q 8 5 4
◇ Q 3
♣ K 9 7

South *(Billy)*
♠ 10
♡ —
◇ J 9 8 7 6 2
♣ A Q J 10 8 6

West	North	East	South
	1♠	pass	2◇
4♡	4NT	5♡	6◇!
pass	?		

Slowly, very slowly, I reviewed our responses to interrupted Blackwood. A double would show 0 or 3, a pass would show 1 or 4, 5♠ (the next suit) would show 2 and 5NT (the next step after 5♠) would show 2 with the queen. But 6◇? Why does he do this to me? Why doesn't he let me be the one to make up new bids in the heat of battle (which I like to do). In a fit of anger I bid 7◇.

Imagine my misery when West led the ♡A. Imagine my relief when Billy trumped it. Imagine my misery when Billy couldn't claim after drawing trumps. Imagine my joy when the club finesse worked. 'What was that 6◇ bid supposed to mean?' I asked.

It turned out Billy had made up a new response to show an ace plus a void. Sure Billy, I knew exactly what you were doing.

My good friend Walter Bingham, senior editor for Sports
Illustrated, *plays bridge on the commuter train every day to
and from work in New York city. He always has these 'train'
stories to tell me.*

Six if by train

Neither vul.

North
♠ Q J 4
♡ A 8 7 4
◇ Q
♣ A K Q J 10

West
♠ 10 9 8 7 6
♡ K Q J 10 6 5
◇ 4 3
♣ —

East
♠ —
♡ 9 3 2
◇ K 9 8 7 6 5
♣ 7 6 4 3

South (Walter)
♠ A K 5 3 2
♡ —
◇ A J 10 2
♣ 9 8 5 2

West	North	East	South
		3◇	pass
pass	dbl	pass	4♠
pass	6♠	all pass	

Opening lead: ♡K

True, 7♣ is a better contract, but 6♠ isn't exactly chopped
liver. In any case Walter won the opening lead, discarding a
diamond, and played the ♠Q getting the bad news.
Undaunted, he ran the ◇Q and then played three more
rounds of trumps, leaving West with the high trump. Walter
then led a club from his hand and West hesitated. Walter,
thinking it did not matter when West trumped in, showed
his cards. East saw at once that if West ruffed the fourth
club and got out with a heart, Walter would be stuck with a
diamond loser.

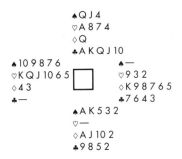

♠Q J 4
♡A 8 7 4
♢Q
♣A K Q J 10

♠10 9 8 7 6
♡K Q J 10 6 5
♢4 3
♣—

♠—
♡9 3 2
♢K 9 8 7 6 5
♣7 6 4 3

♠A K 5 3 2
♡—
♢A J 10 2
♣9 8 5 2

West, not such a good player, also realized that he might be able to do something. After taking a good look at Walter's hand, he said, 'I am going to ruff the third club.' He had forgotten that Walter had already led a club. When he looked at Walter's hand, he saw three clubs.

Pity. West ruffed the third club and played a heart. Walter ruffed and was able to pitch his losing diamond on dummy's fifth club. So much for premature claims.

Can you see how the slam can be made legitimately? Ruff the opening lead; cross to the ♠Q; run the ♢Q; draw three more rounds of trumps, discarding a heart from the table; cash the ♢A, discarding dummy's last small heart, and start with the clubs. Whenever West ruffs, he must return a heart to dummy's ace and dummy is high.

'Yes, I do have that many'

How to handle a nine-card suit? Bid it, bid it again, and then bid it some more. Here's the story of one nine-card suit from a National Championship.

Neither vul.

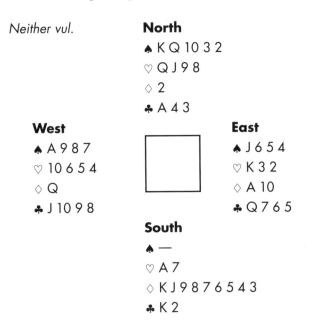

North
♠ K Q 10 3 2
♡ Q J 9 8
♢ 2
♣ A 4 3

West
♠ A 9 8 7
♡ 10 6 5 4
♢ Q
♣ J 10 9 8

East
♠ J 6 5 4
♡ K 3 2
♢ A 10
♣ Q 7 6 5

South
♠ —
♡ A 7
♢ K J 9 8 7 6 5 4 3
♣ K 2

West	North	East	South
	1♠	pass	2◇
pass	2♡	pass	5◇
pass	pass	pass	

Opening lead: ♣J

It goes without saying that nobody in the South seat knew exactly how to handle this hand. One pair wound up in 3NT and made zillions when declarer guessed the diamonds correctly leading low to the king. Others wound up in 6◇, which can be made if South wins the club lead, takes the heart finesse and then guesses diamonds correctly.

When I held the South hand, I jump-shifted to 3◇ but was afraid to put that in the bidding diagram; 11 HCP jump shifts are not everyone's cup of tea. Strangely, after jump-shifting I wound up in five diamonds whereas many who responded 2◇ wound up in slam! Playing 5◇ with a club lead presents some problems, as you only have one dummy entry. Should you use it to finesse hearts or should you use it to lead up to your diamond holding. After all leading a diamond from dummy works if East has a singleton ace, a singleton queen or a doubleton A-Q. On the other hand, finessing in hearts works if East has the king no matter how the diamonds lie as long as West doesn't have all of the missing diamonds (if he did, his double would have shaken the room).

The correct play in five diamonds on a club lead is to win in dummy and take the heart finesse. Even if the finesse loses, you still have a chance to get the diamonds right by plunking down the king (picks up a singleton queen) or by leading a low diamond (picking off a singleton ace). If you lead a diamond at Trick 2 and get it wrong, you are doomed to lose two diamonds and a heart.

Have you ever had an overwhelming desire to put a bidding theory to the test even though it means making a bid partner may not read? Well, I once tried it in the finals of the U.S team playoffs and look what happened.

Both vul.

North
- ♠ 4
- ♡ A K J 10 7 6
- ◊ K 2
- ♣ 10 6 4 2

West
- ♠ A K
- ♡ 3
- ◊ 9 8 7 4
- ♣ K Q 9 8 7 5

East
- ♠ Q J 6 3 2
- ♡ Q 9 8 5 2
- ◊ 10 5 3
- ♣ —

South (Theorist?)
- ♠ 10 9 8 7 5
- ♡ 4
- ◊ A Q J 6
- ♣ A J 3

West	North	East	South
			1◊!
2♣	2♡	pass	2♠
pass	3♣	pass	3NT
all pass			

Opening lead: ♣K

I know the finals of the U.S international team playoffs is not the place to test theories, but the South hand presented too much of a temptation. I opened the South hand 1◊ instead of 1♠. It seems to me that rebidding problems will be easier over partner's expected heart response if I start with 1◊. Furthermore, if I open 1♠ and partner responds 2♡, what is to become of me? I am not enamored with rebidding a five-card suit headed by a ten-spot and partner and I were playing that a 2NT rebid showed a little extra.

After my reverse(!) and partner's groping 3♣, I bid 3NT and there we were. I grabbed the opening lead and led a heart to the jack and queen. At this point I was sure they were going to cash three or four spade tricks along with the ♣K and beat me a trick or two. Worse, it looked like 4♡ could be made (it couldn't). I was planning my apologies; it turned out I didn't have to.

After winning the ♡Q, East, never dreaming I had five spades, shifted to the ♠Q. With the spades blocked, the opponents could only take four tricks: two spades, one heart and one club. In the meantime, I had nine tricks: four diamonds, three hearts and two clubs. So was I lucky or a genius? My partner didn't have any trouble answering that one.

Can you imagine being talked into playing that a raise from 2NT to 3NT is a transfer to 4♣ and in order to raise to 3NT naturally you have to bid 3♠? Well, my partner, Marshall Miles, convinced me that this was the 'only' way to play over 2NT, so I agreed to try it.

Try it, you'll like it

Both vul.

North
- ♠ Q 4
- ♡ 7 6
- ◇ A J 10 7 6 3 2
- ♣ 5 4

West
- ♠ 10 8 7
- ♡ Q J 10 8
- ◇ Q 9
- ♣ Q 10 8 6

East
- ♠ J 6 5 2
- ♡ 9 5 3 2
- ◇ 5
- ♣ A J 9 2

South
- ♠ A K 9 3
- ♡ A K 4
- ◇ K 8 4
- ♣ K 7 3

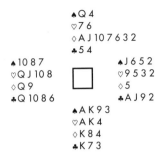

```
            ♠Q 4
            ♡7 6
            ♦A J 10 7 6 3 2
            ♣5 4
♠10 8 7                    ♠J 6 5 2
♡Q J 10 8                  ♡9 5 3 2
♦Q 9                       ♦5
♣Q 10 8 6                  ♣A J 9 2
            ♠A K 9 3
            ♡A K 4
            ♦K 8 4
            ♣K 7 3
```

So here we are playing the 'system' in a National Swiss Team event and on the last day of this ten-day tournament Marshall finally opens 2NT on the South hand shown here. By that time I couldn't even remember the 'normal' responses to 2NT let alone Marshall's new advanced method. My proper response (I think) was 4♣ (a transfer to diamonds) and then I could show slam inclination by bidding something or other which, of course, I had forgotten.

At the time, none of that entered my mind and I bid a simple 3NT and hoped for the best. Keep in mind I have just made a transfer to clubs and I have seven diamonds! Marshall alerted my bid as a transfer and I was beginning to wonder how many times I would have to bid diamonds to convince Marshall that I had had a 'memory lapse'. I also tried my best not to give away to Marshall what I had done.

Lo and behold, Marshall continued with his explanation of my 3NT bid. He said, 'It is supposed to show clubs, but I don't believe it; pass.' Well, I could have jumped across the table and kissed Marshall for figuring out that I had actually forgotten his beloved convention.

But as the play started, I began to realize that something had gone awry. Marshall won the opening heart lead, cashed the ◇K and when both opponents followed, he had twelve tricks. Not content with twelve, Marshall made thirteen. He cashed a second high heart and then ran all seven diamonds. On the last diamond East had four spades and the blank ace of clubs and Marshall had four spades and the blank king of clubs. Unfortunately for him, East had to discard before Marshall. When he let go of a spade, Marshall discarded his ♣K and took the last four spade tricks to make seven! That scoundrel Miles had passed my transfer response and we had missed a cold slam!

'Marshall, I said, 'the least you can do is honor my transfer bids — or did you forget?' Silence.

Some hands fill you with a pleasant afterglow. The setting was Geneva, Switzerland, and Billy Eisenberg and I had been invited to play as a team with Benito Garozzo and Giorgio Belladonna (we had asked them to get us strong teammates, but that was the best they could do) against a Swiss International Team. This was far and away my favorite deal of the match, which we won by a small margin, to some extent due to what happened here.

If you can't beat them, join them

Both vul.

North
♠ 5 4
♡ K Q 5 4
◇ 8 4
♣ A Q 9 8 3

West (me)
♠ 8 7 6
♡ J 10 7 6
◇ Q J 10 6 5 3
♣ —

East (Billy)
♠ A J 10 3 2
♡ 2
◇ K 9 2
♣ J 10 7 6

South
♠ K Q 9
♡ A 9 8 3
◇ A 7
♣ K 5 4 2

West	North	East	South
			1NT
pass	2♣	pass	2♡
pass	4♡	all pass	

Opening lead: ◇Q

Actually 6♡ is not a bad contract. If hearts are 3-2 and clubs don't break obscenely, you have twelve tricks. You win the diamond lead, draw trumps, pitch a diamond from your hand on dummy's fifth club and concede the ♠A. Look at what happened to this declarer when both clubs *and* hearts broke obscenely.

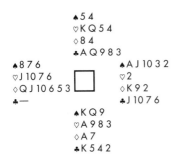

```
            ♠ 5 4
            ♡ K Q 5 4
            ◇ 8 4
            ♣ A Q 9 8 3
♠ 8 7 6                   ♠ A J 10 3 2
♡ J 10 7 6                ♡ 2
◇ Q J 10 6 5 3            ◇ K 9 2
♣ —                       ♣ J 10 7 6
            ♠ K Q 9
            ♡ A 9 8 3
            ◇ A 7
            ♣ K 5 4 2
```

South won the opening lead, Billy signaling with the ◇9 to show the king. South continued with three rounds of trumps, Billy discarding two spades. When declarer played the ♣K, I decided not to ruff, pitching a spade, and when declarer continued with a second club to dummy's ace, I pitched a second spade. At this point declarer decided to lead a low spade from dummy, a play he was soon to regret, big time.

Billy, alive to the position, jumped up with the ace and underled his ◇K to my ten. I was now able to cash the ♡J, taking away both dummy's and declarer's last trump. We were now playing notrump. Now get a load of this. On my ♡J, Billy discarded the ◇K! Now all of my diamonds were good and we took the rest of the tricks. Down four!

In the other room Garozzo wound up in 4♡, losing the inevitable trick in each suit with the marked diamond lead. Billy and I learned one thing from this match — it was far better to play with Garozzo and Belladonna as teammates than to play against them.

Cardiac arrest hand

This is a serious question. Say you pick up this jewel of a hand in the East seat:

♠ 5 4 3 2   ♡ 7   ◇ 5 4 3 2   ♣ 5 4 3 2

Your partner, West, leads the ♠K against South's contract of 7♡ and you take the setting trick with the ♡7. Yes, you are reading correctly. Not only that, but declarer is an expert and is playing the hand properly. Can you construct a hand to fit these conditions?

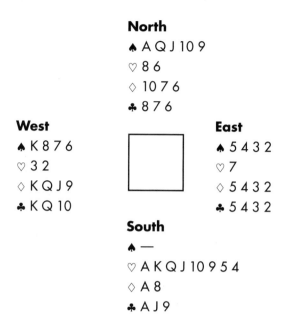

North
- ♠ A Q J 10 9
- ♡ 8 6
- ◇ 10 7 6
- ♣ 8 7 6

West
- ♠ K 8 7 6
- ♡ 3 2
- ◇ K Q J 9
- ♣ K Q 10

East
- ♠ 5 4 3 2
- ♡ 7
- ◇ 5 4 3 2
- ♣ 5 4 3 2

South
- ♠ —
- ♡ A K Q J 10 9 5 4
- ◇ A 8
- ♣ A J 9

Here is a possible construction. West leads the ◇K against a 7♡ contract. The only legitimate play is to try to establish the spades via a trump finesse, which means digging up two dummy entries in hearts — one to get to the spades, one to use them after they are established. Translation: you have to find West with the ♡7 (the percentage play for two entries is to lead low to the six hoping to find West with 7-x or 7-x-x) and East with the ♠K.

Assuming you haven't fainted, or worse, when you take the second trick with the ♡7 you can return a diamond (or a club) and defeat the contract two tricks. Reverse the East-West hands and South makes the grand. Win some, lose some. By the way, this is a great problem to give someone on your A list; it is guaranteed you won't hear from this person for a while.

A thing of beauty

Conventions, conventions, conventions. They are so great and yet so dangerous. What's so dangerous about them? For openers, have you ever been involved in a sequence where either you or your partner makes what he or she thinks is a conventional bid while the other has either completely forgotten the convention or doesn't think that it is a conventional bid? No matter how it turns out, it usually leads to a good story.

Both vul.

North
- ♠ Q 10 8 3
- ♡ Q
- ♢ K Q 8 7 6
- ♣ 10 4 3

West
- ♠ A 9 2
- ♡ J 7 6
- ♢ J 5 2
- ♣ Q J 5 2

East
- ♠ 4
- ♡ K 5 4 3 2
- ♢ A 10 9 4 3
- ♣ 8 7

South
- ♠ K J 7 6 5
- ♡ A 10 9 8
- ♢ —
- ♣ A K 9 6

West	North	East	South
			1♠
pass	3♠	pass	4♡
pass	4NT	pass	5NT
pass	6♣	pass	6♠
all pass			

Opening lead: ♡6

Do not try to understand the bidding. You are going to need an explanation. I was South, playing with Bob Hamman (now the world's #1 ranking player), both in our youth. His

3♠ was a limit raise and Bob was under the impression that my 4♡ bid was an asking bid, asking what he had in hearts. I, on the other hand, was innocently cuebidding my ♡A, not thinking that this was one of our 'asking bid' sequences. Why didn't I cuebid 4♣? Good question. I think I was planning on bidding 5♣ over 4♠ to pinpoint the diamond void. Not sure.

Anyway, Bob's 4NT bid showed second-round heart control, only I thought it was Blackwood. My response of 5NT showed two aces and a void. (At that time neither one of us had ever heard of Keycard Blackwood). When I bid 5NT he thought it was the Grand Slam Force asking about *his* trump holding (was this a well-knit partnership, or what?). His 6♣ bid showed weak trumps. Of course, I didn't know that. I thought he was asking *me* about how good my trumps were! I decided they weren't so hot and bid 6♠ which Bob passed, mercifully. I told you that a bidding explanation was needed. Now on to the play.

For some reason best known to West, he decided to lead a heart. East was reluctant to stick up the king (it wouldn't matter) and dummy's queen held. At Trick 2 I tried the ◇K, covered by the ace and ruffed. My ♡A allowed me to pitch a club from dummy and a heart was ruffed. The ◇Q was cashed as I pitched a club. Next, I entered my hand with the ♣A, ruffed my last heart, ruffed a diamond low, cashed the ♣K and ruffed my remaining club. At this point I remained with the K-J-7 of spades and partner had the stiff queen of spades and two little diamonds. All they could take was the ♠A.

I ask you this: was this, or was this not, a beautifully bid slam?

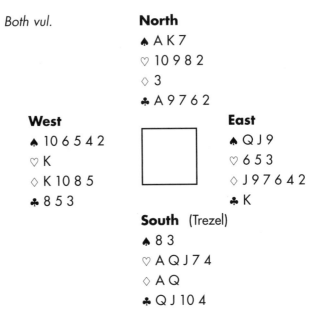

Femme fatale

As the story goes, the famous French player, Roger Trezel, was sitting South playing in a tournament against a lady in the West seat who was wearing a low-cut dress. This was the first of two boards.

Both vul.

North
♠ A K 7
♡ 10 9 8 2
♢ 3
♣ A 9 7 6 2

West
♠ 10 6 5 4 2
♡ K
♢ K 10 8 5
♣ 8 5 3

East
♠ Q J 9
♡ 6 5 3
♢ J 9 7 6 4 2
♣ K

South (Trezel)
♠ 8 3
♡ A Q J 7 4
♢ A Q
♣ Q J 10 4

West	North	East	South
			1♡
pass	2♣	pass	3♣
pass	3♡	pass	4♢
pass	6♡	all pass	

Opening lead: ♣3

Trezel, fearing a singleton lead, went up with the ♣A intending to rely on the heart finesse to make the slam. Lo and behold, when he played the ace the singleton king of clubs fell from East! Trezel had it right, sort of; *somebody* had a singleton.

Now there was no need to risk the heart finesse, as there was a great danger that if the finesse lost, the lady would give her partner a club ruff. Trezel simply played the ♡A and guess what? The singleton king of hearts fell from West! Trezel made seven, losing to neither singleton king! Later, he overheard his right-hand opponent, shaken from losing both kings, discussing the hand. 'From the moment we sat down at the table, that young man was craning his neck looking unashamedly into my partner's cards. No wonder we didn't make either king.'

Former Dallas Ace and writer extraordinaire, Mike Lawrence, played the following deal during a Knockout Team of Four Championship at the Ambassador Hotel in Los Angeles partnered by the late Bobby Goldman, also a former Dallas Ace.

How to Read Your Opponents' Cards

Both vul.

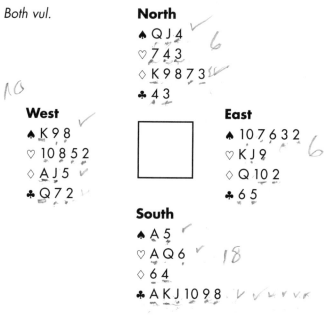

North
♠ Q J 4
♡ 7 4 3
♦ K 9 8 7 3
♣ 4 3

West
♠ K 9 8
♡ 10 8 5 2
♦ A J 5
♣ Q 7 2

East
♠ 10 7 6 3 2
♡ K J 9
♦ Q 10 2
♣ 6 5

South
♠ A 5
♡ A Q 6
♦ 6 4
♣ A K J 10 9 8

West	North	East	South
			1♣
pass	1♦	pass	3NT
all pass			

Opening lead: ♦A!

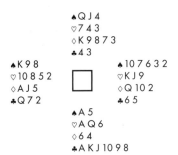

♠Q J 4
♡7 4 3
♢K 9 8 7 3
♣4 3

♠K 9 8
♡10 8 5 2
♢A J 5
♣Q 7 2

♠10 7 6 3 2
♡K J 9
♢Q 10 2
♣6 5

♠A 5
♡A Q 6
♢6 4
♣A K J 10 9 8

The reason for the seemingly strange lead was the fact that the 3NT rebid promised a strong hand with long clubs plus outside stoppers. The 3NT bidder frequently has a singleton in partner's suit, possibly a void. Not this time.

West continued with the ♢J to dummy's king. Lawrence tried a losing club finesse and West exited with a third diamond to East as Lawrence discarded a heart. East now produced the three of spades.

The moment of truth had arrived. Should he allow the lead to run to dummy where a couple of high diamonds resided? If East had the ♠K, all of Lawrence's troubles would be over. But what if West had the king? He would win and exit with a spade (or a club) and Mike would be stuck in his hand with a losing heart. But why would East lead a spade from the king when a heart return looked so much more inviting?

Lawrence hasn't won three World Championships for nothing. He had no trouble with the spade return. He won the ace, cashed his clubs and exited with a spade to West's king. West was stuck. He either had to lead a spade to dummy's queen or lead a heart into Mike's A-Q. 3NT bid and made.

One of my favorite Mike Lawrence stories involves a hand he bid with Harold Guiver. They had agreed upon several suits and it was clear they were heading for a grand in one of them. Rather than make the choice himself, Mike bid 7♣ (clubs were an unbid suit) on a singleton ace, waiting for Harold to choose. Harold, holding the Q-x-x of clubs, thought he had the golden holding in clubs, and passed!

When Harold put the dummy down he hid the ♣Q under one of his clubs trying to scare Mike. When he finally uncovered the queen, he said 'And look at this nice little surprise I have for you.' Mike replied: 'Oh, you clever little devil, you'.

How would you like to be playing on VuGraph with hundreds of people watching your every move? Could be nerve-wracking for some, but apparently not for Montreal expert Sam Gold. When he played this deal, hundreds were looking on; hundreds who could see all four hands.

Gold dust

N-S vul.

North
- ♠ A
- ♡ A 10 8 4
- ◇ K 7 4
- ♣ A J 7 6 5

West
- ♠ 8 6 2
- ♡ K J 7 5 2
- ◇ J 8 6 5 3
- ♣ —

East
- ♠ K J 10 5 3
- ♡ 6
- ◇ A
- ♣ Q 10 9 4 3 2

South (Gold)
- ♠ Q 9 7 4
- ♡ Q 9 3
- ◇ Q 10 9 2
- ♣ K 8

West	North	East	South
		1♣	pass
1♡	pass	1♠	pass
pass	dbl	pass	1NT
2◇	dbl	2♠	2NT
pass	3NT	all pass	

Opening lead: ♠8

Gold's judgment was excellent inasmuch as it led to a vulnerable game rather than to a penalty double of 2♠, which is down one or two depending upon the defense — even with a trump lead. As Gold studied the dummy, the commentators pointed out how the hand could be made if declarer never touched a wrong card. Gold followed the

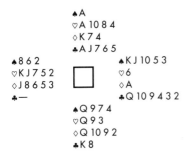

```
              ♠ A
              ♡ A 10 8 4
              ◇ K 7 4
              ♣ A J 7 6 5
♠ 8 6 2                      ♠ K J 10 5 3
♡ K J 7 5 2                  ♡ 6
◇ J 8 6 5 3                  ◇ A
♣ —                         ♣ Q 10 9 4 3 2
              ♠ Q 9 7 4
              ♡ Q 9 3
              ◇ Q 10 9 2
              ♣ K 8
```

script as if he had been reading their minds.

Dummy's ace won the opening lead, and a low diamond went to East's ace, more or less confirming the distribution that Gold pictured from the bidding. East returned the ♠J to Gold's queen and Sam next ran the ◇10 through West. When this held, a diamond was led to the king, and the ♡A cashed, removing East's lone heart. Gold reentered his hand with the ♣K, cashed the ◇Q, his seventh trick, and exited with a high spade. East scored his three remaining spades, but had to concede the last two tricks to the ♣A-J in dummy. The audience went wild.

Those that do and those that don't

There's an old saying around Los Angeles that the bridge players who wind up on Main Street downtown (the slum area), sitting with a hat in their lap are those players who never drew trumps. Of course, the ones on the opposite side of the street are the ones who drew trumps too quickly.

Both vul.

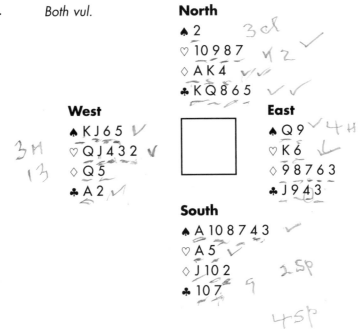

```
              North
              ♠ 2
              ♡ 10 9 8 7
              ◇ A K 4
              ♣ K Q 8 6 5

West                      East
♠ K J 6 5                 ♠ Q 9
♡ Q J 4 3 2               ♡ K 6
◇ Q 5                     ◇ 9 8 7 6 3
♣ A 2                     ♣ J 9 4 3

              South
              ♠ A 10 8 7 4 3
              ♡ A 5
              ◇ J 10 2
              ♣ 10 7
```

West	North	East	South
			2♠

all pass

Opening lead: ♡Q

This is a deal that will stay with me for quite some time. I was South playing with Paul Soloway against Norman Kay, West, and Edgar Kaplan, East, in a quarterfinal Spingold Cup match in Chicago.

I captured the opening lead with the ace, and led a club to the king which held. Obsessed with getting rid of my diamond loser on a club (so far it had been a very bad year for finesses), I exited dummy with a heart trying to 'open up the lines of communication'. Always a good reason to use in the post-mortem. Believe me I needed one. This is what happened.

Edgar won the ♡K and returned a club to Norman's ace. Norman exited with a low heart which Edgar ruffed with the ♠Q and I overruffed with the ace. I now exited with the ♠8 (the ten would have worked better), and Edgar won the nine and returned a club. I ruffed this with the ♠7 and Norman cleverly discarded a diamond.

In case you have lost track, my remaining spades were the 10-4-3 and Norman was sitting over there with the K-J-6. Hoping the spades were now 2-1, I exited with a low spade! Norman took three spade tricks and then two more heart tricks for down three with the ◇Q onside all along!

As the hearts were being run, I heard Paul's voice from across the table: 'Have a little accident, Edwin?'

At least I know which side of Main Street to sit on.

Do what I say, not what I do

At the beginning of many of my classes I ask if anyone has any questions. The most common questions deal with freak hands that they have held since the previous class. Somehow someone always seems to get an eight- or a nine-card suit. I try to stay clear of freak hands by announcing that they don't come up often enough to worry about. Besides, whenever I get one, something terrible usually happens... to me. I then produce the following deal:

E-W vul.

North
- ♠ A K J 4
- ♡ 8 7 6
- ◇ A 8 4
- ♣ J 10 6

West
- ♠ 10 6 5
- ♡ K Q 3
- ◇ J 9 3 2
- ♣ K 9 4

East
- ♠ Q 9 8 7 3 2
- ♡ 2
- ◇ —
- ♣ A Q 8 5 3 2

South
- ♠ —
- ♡ A J 10 9 5 4
- ◇ K Q 10 7 6 5
- ♣ 7

West	North	East	South
			1♡
pass	2NT[1]	pass[2]	3◇
pass	3♡	pass	6♡[3]
pass	pass	dbl[4]	all pass

1. Should have bid 1♠ but likes to play all hands.

2. After a slight hitch. I think passing with a 6-6 hand is worth more than just a slight hitch, don't you?

3. Playing 'God' (that's me, by the way).

4. Hoping to attract a diamond lead.

After the heart preference I decided to keep my hand a secret because I had all of these surprises. Notice who doubled. Not West, the player with the two trump tricks, but his partner East, who was praying for an unusual lead. Doubles of slam contracts call for unusual leads. West worked out that a diamond was the most unusual lead he could come up with and sure enough East ruffed and cashed the ♣A. I still had to lose two more trump tricks for a resounding down three.

So much for asking the teacher about how to handle freak hands.

When you play professionally with clients you soon learn to expect anything. But even I wasn't ready for this!

Playing pro

Neither vul.

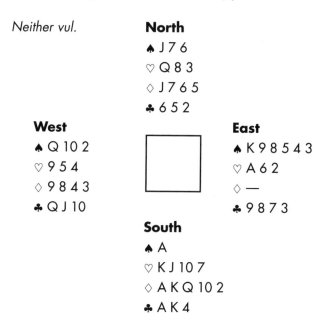

North
- ♠ J 7 6
- ♡ Q 8 3
- ◇ J 7 6 5
- ♣ 6 5 2

West
- ♠ Q 10 2
- ♡ 9 5 4
- ◇ 9 8 4 3
- ♣ Q J 10

East
- ♠ K 9 8 5 4 3
- ♡ A 6 2
- ◇ —
- ♣ 9 8 7 3

South
- ♠ A
- ♡ K J 10 7
- ◇ A K Q 10 2
- ♣ A K 4

The bidding is going to need a 'little' explanation, but first the setting. I am South playing in an evening duplicate with a paying customer. Furthermore, both East and West regularly attend my classes.

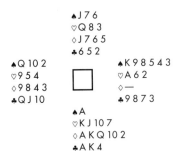

```
          ♠J76
          ♡Q83
          ◊J765
          ♣652
♠Q102              ♠K98543
♡954               ♡A62
◊9843              ◊—
♣QJ10              ♣9873
          ♠A
          ♡KJ107
          ◊AKQ102
          ♣AK4
```

My partner is only comfortable playing strong twos so I opened 2◊. My partner gave me the positive response of 3◊ (2NT is the correct way to show this kind of hand), and I was off to the races. I bid 4NT to ask for aces and my partner responded 5◊ as a signoff. I thought he had an ace and bid 7◊. East, with the ace my partner was supposed to have, decided not to double and there we were.

When the dummy came down, I didn't say anything, but I thought to myself, 'It's going to be a long evening.' I won the opening lead and banged down the ◊A only to see East discard a high spade. Suddenly a glimmer of hope appeared. Now the pairs in 6◊ would likely be going down one trick, so if I could just figure out a way to go down only one, I could salvage a few matchpoints. I hatched a plan.

If I could ruff two spades in my hand, I could reverse the dummy and discard a losing club on dummy's fourth diamond. Of course, I would need a little help. I cashed the ♠A and led the ♡K. East won the ace and played a high spade which I ruffed. Just what the doctor ordered. In order to complete this coup, I need two more dummy entries. I would have to lead the seven of hearts to dummy's eight, ruff another spade, cash my two high diamonds, reenter dummy with the ♡Q and play the ◊J discarding my club. Down one. Of course for all of this to happen West needed the nine of hearts and had to have at least three hearts.

If you check the diagram, you will see that my plan was going to work and I would have a deal I could write up. Of course when I wrote about it, I would be playing 6◊ so I could make my contract. Anyway, I led the ♡7 and what do you think happened? This lady from my class, sitting West, covered with the nine! I no longer had two dummy entries, could not reverse the dummy, and had to go down two.

There must be a more enjoyable way to make a living, but I haven't found it yet.

Have you read any books on defensive card play suggesting that when you have supported partner with a weak hand holding something like Kxxx(x) or Qxxx(x) in partner's suit that you should lead your honor instead of a low card? The rationale is that since you have a weak hand, you may never regain the lead if you lead low, whereas if you lead high and your honor takes the trick you may be able to make a killing switch at Trick 2. Burn those books.

Neither vul.

North
- ♠ A J 10 8
- ♡ A 7 4
- ◇ 10 9 3
- ♣ K 10 6

West
- ♠ K 5 3 2
- ♡ 10 9 3 2
- ◇ Q J 6 4
- ♣ 2

East
- ♠ Q 9 7 6 4
- ♡ K J 8
- ◇ A K 2
- ♣ 7 4

South
- ♠ —
- ♡ Q 6 5
- ◇ 8 7 5
- ♣ A Q J 9 8 5 3

West	North	East	South
		1♠	4♣
4♠	5♣	dbl	all pass

Opening lead: ?

It was my lead and I had read all the wrong books — even one I had written suggesting the high honor lead with a weak hand. This seemed like the perfect occasion. I led the ♠K, the only card in my hand that allows the contract to come home.

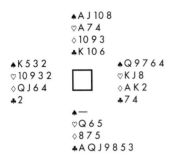

```
           ♠ A J 10 8
           ♥ A 7 4
           ♦ 10 9 3
           ♣ K 10 6
♠ K 5 3 2              ♠ Q 9 7 6 4
♥ 10 9 3 2            ♥ K J 8
♦ Q J 6 4             ♦ A K 2
♣ 2                   ♣ 7 4
           ♠ —
           ♥ Q 6 5
           ♦ 8 7 5
           ♣ A Q J 9 8 5 3
```

If I lead a diamond, we beat the hand two tricks. If I lead a heart or a low spade we beat the hand one trick (declarer can pitch a diamond on the ♠A), but watch what happened when I led the ♠K. Declarer won the ace, discarding a diamond and then played the ♠J. My partner ducked (correctly), and off went another diamond. (Thank God the dummy didn't have the A-J-10-9 of spades or else declarer could have gotten rid of all three of his diamonds!) When the smoke cleared, South wound up losing one diamond and one heart; I wound up losing one partner and destroying three bridge books.

A Greek gift

Sometimes a simple lesson hand turns out to be not so simple after all.

Both vul.

North
♠ J 10 6 3
♥ K Q J 4
♦ —
♣ K Q J 5 2

West
♠ K Q 8 7
♥ 6 2
♦ J 10 9 8 7
♣ 6 4

East
♠ 5 2
♥ A 10 9 8
♦ A 6 5 3 2
♣ 7 3

South
♠ A 9 4
♥ 7 5 3
♦ K Q 4
♣ A 10 9 8

West	North	East	South
			1♣
pass	1♡	pass	1NT
pass	2♠	pass	2NT
pass	5♣	all pass	

Opening lead: ◇J

Well, it's not an easy hand to bid and the way the cards lie (◇A with East), 3NT would be easy. However, 5♣ it was. The diamond lead was not a good idea. Dummy was surely short in diamonds and South was known to have diamond strength given the 2NT rebid; a trump would have been a better idea.

The question is: how should South play this hand in 5♣? If South ruffs the opening lead and drives out the ♡A after drawing a couple of trumps, East will return a spade and, with hearts breaking 4-2 and both spades lurking in the wrong hand, the hand is destined for a one-trick set.

But wait! What if a spade is discarded from dummy at Trick 1? Say East wins and returns a spade. Too late. South wins the ace, draws trumps, discards two more spades from dummy on the K-Q of diamonds, and winds up losing two red aces but no spades. Making five.

But wait! What if East doesn't play the ◇A at Trick 1? You got it, the hand can't be made. South still has to lose two spades and one heart. So what does this hand teach us? It teaches us that from declarer's point of view, it is definitely right to discard a spade from dummy at Trick 1 with these combined spade and diamond holdings. Most East players will grab the ◇A thinking they have just been given a present from heaven. However, a strong East player who knows what you are up to will play low at Trick 1 exchanging his ◇A for two spade tricks. Tuck that one away.

A rare gem

This column will surely please the expert, but may go over the head of the novice. Nonetheless, it is a rare and beautiful play that most experts will admit they have never encountered.

E-W vul.

North
♠ A Q 7 6
♡ K 9 3
◇ Q 6
♣ K 8 7 3

West
♠ K 9 8 5 4
♡ 8 2
◇ K 10 8 3 2
♣ 2

East
♠ J 10
♡ 10 7 4
◇ A 9 5 4
♣ Q J 10 4

South
♠ 3 2
♡ A Q J 6 5
◇ J 7
♣ A 9 6 5

West	North	East	South
			1♡
pass	1♠	pass	2♣
pass	3♡	pass	4♡
all pass			

Opening lead: ◇3

East won the opening lead and returned the suit to West's king. West exited with the ♣2. Before reading any further, you might like to try to make this contract looking at all four hands.

There is a way. Win the club in the closed hand, finesse the ♠Q, cash the ace and ruff a spade. Now the ace of hearts and a heart to the king followed by dummy's last spade. This is the five-card end position before you lead dummy's spade:

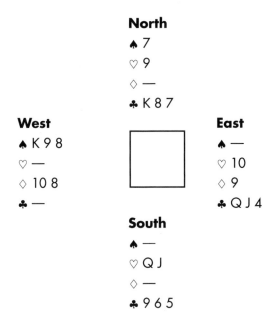

North
♠ 7
♡ 9
♢ —
♣ K 8 7

West
♠ K 9 8
♡ —
♢ 10 8
♣ —

East
♠ —
♡ 10
♢ 9
♣ Q J 4

South
♠ —
♡ Q J
♢ —
♣ 9 6 5

When the spade is led, East has to discard something. If he discards a diamond, South ruffs, draws the last trump and ducks a club into East, who has to return a club ceding declarer the last two tricks.

If East discards a club, South ruffs the spade, cashes the club ace and exits with a club to East. If East returns a heart, South has the rest. If East returns a diamond, South ruffs in dummy and takes the last trick with a high heart.

Finally, if East discards a trump(!), South overruffs and ducks a club into East, who is either endplayed in clubs or has to give South a ruff and a sluff with a diamond lead.

The rarity of the play is that by ruffing spades twice in the South hand, declarer squeezes East out of his safe diamond exit cards, a club winner or a trump and is eventually endplayed in clubs as a result. The hand was played by Bob Hamman, currently the #1 ranked player in the world.

Bravo, Benito

In the 1960s, opinion was fairly evenly divided as to who was the best player in the world (present company excepted, of course). The names of Terence Reese of England and Pietro Forquet of Italy were mentioned frequently. Yet one was just beginning to hear mention of a dark horse in the running: Forquet's partner, Benito Garozzo. With this hand as an example of his 'normal' play, he started to move right to the top of the list.

Neither vul.

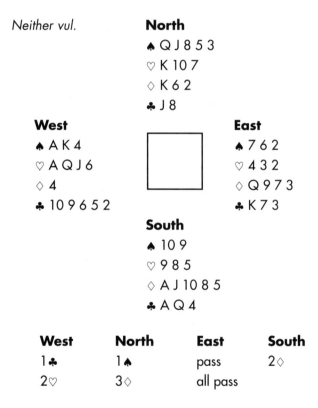

North
♠ Q J 8 5 3
♡ K 10 7
◇ K 6 2
♣ J 8

West
♠ A K 4
♡ A Q J 6
◇ 4
♣ 10 9 6 5 2

East
♠ 7 6 2
♡ 4 3 2
◇ Q 9 7 3
♣ K 7 3

South
♠ 10 9
♡ 9 8 5
◇ A J 10 8 5
♣ A Q 4

West	North	East	South
1♣	1♠	pass	2◇
2♡	3◇	all pass	

Opening lead: ♣10

Garozzo covered the opening lead with dummy's jack and captured East's king. At Trick 2 a spade went to West's king who hastened to play the A-Q of hearts in an attempt to build up a second heart trick before his ♠A was dislodged. Garozzo won the ♡K and did play a second spade to West. West now cashed the ♡J, the fourth trick for the defense.

It is here that things get interesting. Maybe you should dig out a pen or pencil and start crossing out the cards. This is the seven-card ending,

West to play:

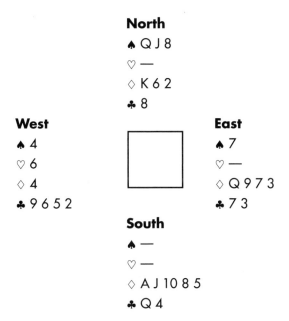

North
♠ Q J 8
♡ —
♢ K 6 2
♣ 8

West
♠ 4
♡ 6
♢ 4
♣ 9 6 5 2

East
♠ 7
♡ —
♢ Q 9 7 3
♣ 7 3

South
♠ —
♡ —
♢ A J 10 8 5
♣ Q 4

At this point West elected to lead his thirteenth heart. A ruff and a sluff frequently works out well in positions where there are no tricks available in the side suits and partner has trump length, but not this time. This time the ♣9 would have defeated the contract. However, the heart lead would have beaten most declarers on this planet, but not Garozzo.

He ruffed in dummy with the six and underruffed with the five when East made his best play of discarding a club. Now Benito discarded his ♣4 on a high spade, led a low diamond to the jack, cashed the ♣Q, entered dummy with the ♢K and took the last two tricks with the A-10 of diamonds.

Bravo, Benito!

Horses for courses

Many years ago, Roosevelt Raceway was once the site of a Regional tournament. The Pari-mutuel windows were used to sell entries. The unusual venue inspired the following anonymous contribution:

Neither vul.

North
♠ A 4 3 2
♡ A 10 8
◇ A K 7 4
♣ K 4

West
♠ 10 6
♡ J 9 5 3
◇ 9 5 2
♣ 9 5 3 2

East
♠ J 9 8 7
♡ 7 6 4 2
◇ Q 8
♣ A J 10

South
♠ K Q 5
♡ K Q
◇ J 10 6 3
♣ Q 8 7 6

West	North	East	South
			1◇
pass	6◇!	all pass	

Opening lead: ◇ 5

Bridge tourney locales are picked for a reason.
Why Roosevelt Raceway? 'Twas the off season.

I turned up in search of a knockout team,
But when this fell through hatched a cunning scheme.

When I asked the Director, they hedged of course,
Cause I chose as my partner, an outstanding horse.

'This is the Mixed Pairs,' I said with glee;
When I put it like that, they had to agree.

The track was fast, the room was hot;
My partner said 'We'll win in a trot.'

Our game got better, I was agog;
My partner said, 'We're home in a jog.'

As we improved, the opponents cried 'foul',
They wanted us to throw in the towel.

Our next opponents were both tournament staff;
Gave them two zeros and the old horse laugh.

Here's the hand, six diamonds is cold;
With a diamond lead, my partner rolled.

He went up with the king, which was quite keen,
Then cashed the ace and caught the queen.

The diamond lead would have been absurd
If West had led from queen empty third.

Without this key, the hook is right:
A lucky lead, our lucky night.

Then half-way through, the clouds really burst;
Our game turned sour and then got worse.

Can't do well in the mud, need a track that's fast;
We broke our stride and were nosed out — for last!

Let it rain next year — my opponents will shudder,
For my new partner will be the world's best mudder.

Mixed Pairs

True story coming up.

N-S vul.

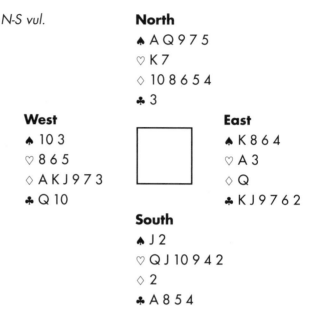

North
- ♠ A Q 9 7 5
- ♡ K 7
- ◊ 10 8 6 5 4
- ♣ 3

West
- ♠ 10 3
- ♡ 8 6 5
- ◊ A K J 9 7 3
- ♣ Q 10

East
- ♠ K 8 6 4
- ♡ A 3
- ◊ Q
- ♣ K J 9 7 6 2

South
- ♠ J 2
- ♡ Q J 10 9 4 2
- ◊ 2
- ♣ A 8 5 4

West	North	East	South
		1♣	1♡
2◊	2♠	dbl	3♡
dbl	all pass		

Opening lead: ◊A

The bidding, which is not all that unusual, comes from a Mixed Pairs event. What was unusual was what happened on the previous deal. On that deal the husband, South, made a play-by-play commentary to his wife as he was stroking home a 1♠ contract, the bidding having gone 1♠ by the husband, all pass. When the dummy came down with a long diamond suit, the husband was aghast and promptly informed his wife she should have mentioned the suit. However, as the play unfolded and he saw that her pass was turning out beautifully, he complimented her on her fine judgment and pointed out that all those who had foolishly bid diamonds with her hand would be getting into trouble.

By now both my partner and I were getting a 'bit' uncomfortable. It's bad enough to get a bottom without being reminded of it three or four times in the same deal. Yearning for revenge I picked up the West hand you see in the diagram. I probably would have doubled this fellow with almost any hand and I certainly wasn't going to let my three little hearts deter me.

After I led the ◇A, the first two cards dummy put down were the K-7 of hearts. 'You have the king of hearts, darling; why I never expected that card,' were South's first words. Next, dummy placed the ace and queen of spades on the table. '*The ace of spades*! Oh, how beautiful, and I'm doubled, ha ha!'

By now the wife was afraid to put down the rest of the dummy for fear it might disappoint her husband. Reluctantly she placed her five little diamonds on the table saying, 'I'm sorry I don't have anything for you in this suit.'

'That's all right dear,' he bellowed, 'I don't have many of those anyway.'

This guy had really gotten to me. Could it be that this fellow was going to make overtricks and I had miscalculated so badly? Finally the singleton club hit the table. 'Dearest, you have a singleton club. Oh, thank you so much.' North was beaming.

I shifted to a low heart at Trick 2. My partner won the king with her ace and continued a heart to South who drew the last trump, my partner discarding the ♠8. Well, I thought, my partner has the spades so what is loudmouth going to do with all of his clubs? I had forgotten about my partner. When declarer led the ♠J at Trick 4, I played the ten trying desperately to show my doubleton. It was all lost on my partner. She took the king and that was our last trick as all of loudmouth's club losers now went off on dummy's spades and my friend in the South seat made an overtrick!

Of course we had it beaten if my partner ducks the ♠J. The best declarer can do is duck a club. But I can win and return a spade and declarer, even if he plays the ace, must lose five tricks: three clubs and two red aces.

Please don't ask me to tell you about the North-South conversation as the hand was being scored. Please.

Listen to the bidding

For a bridge player not to use the bidding as a guide to the play is about as sensible as a doctor ignoring his patient's symptoms as a guide to the cure.

N-S vul.

North
♠ Q 6
♡ A J 3 2
◇ K J 10 4
♣ 10 5 4

West
♠ 7 5
♡ K 10 6
◇ A Q 9 8 2
♣ K Q J

East
♠ J 9 2
♡ 8
◇ 7 6 5
♣ 9 8 7 6 3 2

South
♠ A K 10 8 4 3
♡ Q 9 7 5 4
◇ 3
♣ A

West	North	East	South
			1♠
dbl	redbl	3♣¹	3♡
pass	4♡	pass	4NT²
pass	5◇	pass	6♡
all pass			

1. Preemptive after the redouble.

2. Regular Blackwood.

Opening lead: ♣K

This marginal slam would have been avoided if North-South had been playing Keycard Blackwood, in which the trump king counts as an ace. Notice that North-South have only three of the five keycards, which usually means trouble.

The play of this hand revolves around the trump suit. South cannot afford to lose a heart trick to go along with a diamond trick. Had there been no bidding, the normal play in hearts is low to the jack. If both follow low, the ace is played and on a good day the suit will be 2-2. If East plays the ten under the jack, the closed hand can be reentered to lead the queen through West's king and again, no heart loser.

However, there has been bidding; revealing bidding. West has made a takeout double of one major, more or less guaranteeing support for the other. You should play West for at least three hearts. If he has four hearts or the K-10-8, you are a dead man walking. However, if West has the K-10-6 or the K-8-6 of hearts, you are alive and well.

Lead the ♡Q at Trick 2, which will surely be covered. If East plays the ♡6, you are probably finished as West appears to have K-10-8. However, if East plays the ♡8, re-enter the closed hand to lead the ♡9, repeating the finesse and almost certainly picking up the suit for no losers. As an added bonus, after drawing trumps you will make an overtrick if spades break 3-2 or the jack is singleton, as you can pitch four diamonds from dummy on four spades, eventually ruffing your singleton diamond in dummy!

Chances are not that everyone would think of trumping a diamond in dummy once they see four diamonds over there.

Adam 'Plum' Meredith, British bridge expert non-pareil in the 1950s, was both famous for, and addicted to, bidding three-card spade suits. The bid invariably caused chaos at the table. Sometimes Meredith came out of these adventures smelling like a rose, sometimes not.

E-W vul.

North
♠ A 10 2
♡ 7 5 3 2
◇ A Q 7 4
♣ 8 3

West
♠ K J 9
♡ A K J 4
◇ K J 2
♣ Q J 10

East
♠ 8 7 6 5
♡ Q 10 9 6
◇ 10 9
♣ 6 4 2

South
♠ Q 4 3
♡ 8
◇ 8 6 5 3
♣ A K 9 7 5

West	North	East	South
	pass	pass	1♠[1]
dbl	redbl	2♡	pass
2NT	dbl	pass	3♣
pass	4♠	pass	pass
dbl	all pass		

1. Guess who?

Opening lead: ♡K

Meredith was up to his old tricks and this is what happened: West continued with a second heart was ruffed by declarer. A diamond went to the queen and a second heart ruffed in the closed hand. Dummy was entered with a diamond and now the ♣AK and a club ruff in dummy were followed by a heart ruff in the closed hand, Meredith trumping with his last trump, the queen.

In case you're not counting that's eight tricks in, the lead is in the closed hand and dummy still has the A-10 of spades. Meredith led a club. If West discards, declarer ruffs with the ♠10 and the ♠A is the tenth trick. If West uppercuts dummy with the ♠J, dummy discards and must make two more tricks with the A-10. Four spades doubled, making.

'The only game contract,' observed Meredith as he began to deal the next hand.

Do these things happen to other people or only to me?

Why me?

Neither vul.

North
♠ 10 6 4
♡ A K Q 9 3
◇ A 10 5 4
♣ 7

West
♠ K 8 7 2
♡ 4
◇ 7 3 2
♣ Q 10 5 3 2

East
♠ A 9 3
♡ 10 8 7 6 5
◇ Q 9 8
♣ A 4

South
♠ Q J 5
♡ J 2
◇ K J 6
♣ K J 9 8 6

West	North	East	South
	1♡	pass	2NT
pass	3◇	pass	3NT
all pass			

Opening lead: ♣3

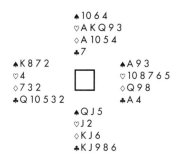

♠ 10 6 4
♡ A K Q 9 3
◇ A 10 5 4
♣ 7

♠ K 8 7 2
♡ 4
◇ 7 3 2
♣ Q 10 5 3 2

♠ A 9 3
♡ 10 8 7 6 5
◇ Q 9 8
♣ A 4

♠ Q J 5
♡ J 2
◇ K J 6
♣ K J 9 8 6

This deal came up in a rubber bridge game at the Cavendish Bridge Club in Los Angeles. East won the club lead and shifted to the three of spades. I played the queen and West won the king and returned the eight of spades. At this point both East and I thought that West had three spades. Anyway, East thought some time and played the nine of spades. I was sure East had the A-9-7-3 of spades and West the K-8-2. Oh well, I wasn't too worried about spades anyway; I had nine tricks and the whole deal was a big joke.

It sure was — on me! I won the ♠J, cashed the ♡J and led a heart to the queen, West discarding a club. Suddenly the hand wasn't a joke. I only had eight tricks! Furthermore, if I misguessed the diamonds, they were (I thought) sure to be able to take two more spade tricks. Rather than commit myself in diamonds, I led a spade from the dummy unblocking the suit for them!

East won the ace and went into a long huddle. I thought he must be thinking of not cashing his winning spade because he wanted me to think his partner had it. If I did, I would finesse the diamond into him and he could then triumphantly produce his winning spade. East returned a club. Well, I thought, this is perfect. I will finesse the club into West and after he wins he will have to return a club or a diamond and I will have my nine tricks back again.

I stuck in the ♣J and after West won the ♣Q, an apparition hit the table, the seven of spades! Not only had I unblocked their spades and misread who had the last spade, but I also had taken a finesse into the danger hand. If word of this hand ever gets out, my reputation, for what it's worth, will be ruined. Please don't tell.

Conventional wisdom says not to reopen with a takeout double over a passed-out one-bid holding a void in the opener's suit. Partner is too apt to pass and since you won't be able to lead a trump or two through declarer, partner will surely be endplayed once or twice at the end of the hand.

E-W vul.

North
♠ 9 4
♡ K J 9 3 2
♢ 8 7 6
♣ 7 6 5

West
♠ A Q J 10 8 3
♡ 10
♢ Q 5
♣ Q 10 3 2

East
♠ —
♡ Q 8 5 4
♢ A 9 4 3 2
♣ A K J 8

South
♠ K 7 6 5 2
♡ A 7 6
♢ K J 10
♣ 9 4

West	North	East	South
			1♠
pass	pass	dbl	all pass

Opening lead: ♠A

When South opened a bit light, my partner, Billy Eisenberg, passed in the West seat as did North. Sitting East in the Grand Nationals finals in Salt Lake City, I decided to reopen with a takeout double, spade void notwithstanding. This is what happened.

Billy made the great lead of the ace of spades and continued with the queen hoping to get in again and draw declarer's trumps. South gulped when he saw me discard a low heart and a low diamond (inferring club strength) at

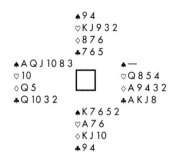

```
              ♠9 4
              ♡K J 9 3 2
              ◇8 7 6
              ♣7 6 5
♠A Q J 10 8 3              ♠—
♡10          ┌───┐        ♡Q 8 5 4
◇Q 5         │   │        ◇A 9 4 3 2
♣Q 10 3 2    └───┘        ♣A K J 8
              ♠K 7 6 5 2
              ♡A 7 6
              ◇K J 10
              ♣9 4
```

Tricks 1 and 2, and took the ♠K. At Trick 3 declarer cashed the ♡A (little did he know that this was his last trick!) and led a heart towards dummy. Billy, alive to what was going on, ruffed the heart, drew declarer's trumps and (now playing notrump) shifted to a club. Four club tricks later saw the hand reduced to two cards with me on lead. I had the A-9 of diamonds, declarer the K-J and Billy the Q-5. I switched to a low diamond, declarer played the jack and we took the last two tricks.

We had defeated the hand five tricks for a score of plus 1400. So much for conventional wisdom.

And hope to die

Promises, promises. Before I played in the World Championships with my partner Billy Eisenberg, he made me swear on my mother's head I would not open a four-card major with a strong hand. In order to preserve the partnership I agreed — with great forebodings. Naturally, playing against the French I picked up the South hand you see below:

N-S vul.

North
♠ J 9 3
♡ 6 5 4 3
◇ 7 6 4
♣ 10 9 2

West
♠ A 10 7 2
♡ 7 2
◇ K Q 9 8
♣ A 7 6

East
♠ Q 6 5
♡ 10 9 8
◇ J 10 3
♣ K J 5 4

South
♠ K 8 4
♡ A K Q J
◇ A 5 2
♣ Q 8 3

West	North	East	South
			1♣
all pass			

Opening lead: ◇K

I gritted my teeth and opened the South hand with 1♣. Never have I felt like such a coward. I was dying to open 1♡. After all, if everyone passes, where do I want to play? So, of course, that is exactly what happened. Vulnerable. And in the World Championship. My promise.

When the smoke cleared I was down three. I couldn't help but notice that I might have made 1♡ or gone down one at most. I didn't know where to vent my rage — at Billy for talking me into that agreement or at myself for going along with it!

At the other table with the French sitting North-South sanity prevailed... but only briefly. The bidding went like this:

West	North	East	South
			1♡
dbl	pass	2♣	pass
pass	2♡!	all pass	

Notice South's intelligent pass over 2♣ (too many losers to get back in the bidding facing a partner who couldn't keep the bidding open), but don't ask me where that 2♡ bid came from. The final contract was defeated two tricks so we only lost 3 IMPs on the board. However, I made myself a solemn promise that I was not going to compromise my principles ever again. When they deal me an AKQJ suit, I'm bidding it! Do you hear me, Billy?

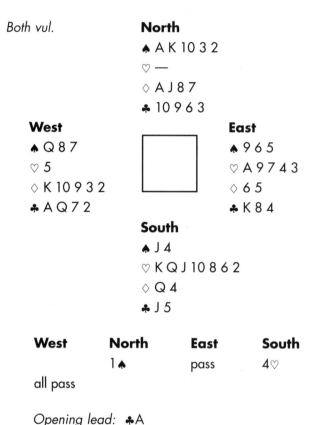

I can dream, can't I?

Some days I play this game so well that I actually frighten myself. Take a look at this deal, for example:

Both vul.

North
♠ A K 10 3 2
♡ —
◊ A J 8 7
♣ 10 9 6 3

West
♠ Q 8 7
♡ 5
◊ K 10 9 3 2
♣ A Q 7 2

East
♠ 9 6 5
♡ A 9 7 4 3
◊ 6 5
♣ K 8 4

South
♠ J 4
♡ K Q J 10 8 6 2
◊ Q 4
♣ J 5

West	North	East	South
	1♠	pass	4♡
all pass			

Opening lead: ♣A

West continued with a low club to the king and East returned a third club. Refusing to believe that West had led from a doubleton club, I ruffed with the six. I continued with the ♡K which held and then the ♡Q which East won, West discarding a diamond. East returned a spade and my jack was covered by West's queen and dummy's king.

As a great player never lets a bad trump break upset him, I set about a trump reduction play. I cashed a second high spade from dummy and ruffed a spade reducing my heart length to East's. It was now a five-card end position. East and I each had three trumps and two diamonds. I led the ◊Q, covered by the king and ace, and led a high spade from dummy; East discarded a diamond as did I. With the lead still in dummy I was able to take the last three tricks with my J-10-8 of hearts hovering over East's 9-7-4.

Now for the real story. Dreading an overruff at Trick 3, I ruffed with the ♡8. The hand is now unmakable because East has two natural trump tricks. Will I always have to wait until the hand is over before I see the winning play?

If you have any ambition to be an expert defender, you must have courage and you must keep counting all of the time. East made a play in this deal that most players wouldn't make if they lived to be a thousand — because he could count.

Count, count, count

Neither vul.

North
♠ J 8 6
♡ 5 4
◇ K J 7 5
♣ A J 10 9

West
♠ 5 3
♡ 2
◇ A Q 10 8 4
♣ Q 8 6 5 3

East
♠ A 10 2
♡ K Q 8 7 6
◇ 9 6 2
♣ K 7

South
♠ K Q 9 7 4
♡ A J 10 9 3
◇ 3
♣ 4 2

West	North	East	South
		1♡	1♠
2◇	2♠	pass	3♠
pass	4♠	all pass	

Opening lead: ♡2

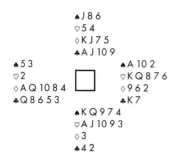

```
            ♠ J 8 6
            ♡ 5 4
            ◇ K J 7 5
            ♣ A J 10 9
♠ 5 3                    ♠ A 10 2
♡ 2          ┌───┐       ♡ K Q 8 7 6
◇ A Q 10 8 4 │   │       ◇ 9 6 2
♣ Q 8 6 5 3  └───┘       ♣ K 7
            ♠ K Q 9 7 4
            ♡ A J 10 9 3
            ◇ 3
            ♣ 4 2
```

West led his singleton and East's queen lost to the ace. A low diamond was led toward dummy and West hopped up with the ace and shifted to a low club.

The ace of clubs and the king of diamonds (South shedding a club) took the next two tricks and then South advanced a heart from dummy. At this point the automatic play is to rise with the ♡K. However, the 'automatic' play won't work. If East takes his king, the most he can take after that is the ♠A and South scores up his game contract.

What happens if East plays a low heart instead? South covers and West ruffs and gets out with a trump. East wins the ace and returns a trump. South can only trump one heart in dummy and has to lose the setting trick to the king of hearts.

How does East know to duck the second round of hearts? East knows that South started with one diamond and probably two clubs. If South had more than two clubs, he would have finessed the ♣J. Even more telling is the opening lead. The lead of the lowest card in a suit partner has bid either shows three (or four) cards or is a singleton. As West has never supported hearts, a major suit that partner has bid, he cannot have heart support. Ergo, the lead must be a singleton. If it is a singleton, it is much wiser to let partner ruff the heart and get out with a trump.

If you want to be an expert, you must be a counter. There is no way of being one without the other.

At one time, many bridge writers used to submit their choice each year for the 'Hand of the Year'. This was an entry from Hugh Kelsey, the late, great Scottish player-writer.

Hand of the Year

N-S vul.

North
♠ A 5
♡ A Q J
◇ A K 8 3
♣ Q 8 6 5

West
♠ 10 9 6
♡ 10 5 4
◇ Q 10 9 5 2
♣ 9 3

East
♠ Q 7 2
♡ K 3
◇ 7 4
♣ K J 10 7 4 2

South
♠ K J 8 4 3
♡ 9 8 7 6 2
◇ J 6
♣ A

West	North	East	South
			pass
pass	1♣	pass	1♠
pass	2NT	pass	3♡
pass	3NT	pass	4♡
pass	5◇	pass	6♡
all pass			

Opening lead: ♣9

The bidding was natural. North's 5◇ bid was a cuebid agreeing hearts as he could hardly be introducing a new suit at this level. South took a chance and bid slam hoping partner's hearts would sustain him.

Declarer won the club opening and immediately led a heart to the jack — which held since John MacLaren, East, ducked the doubleton king! Taken in by this, declarer ruffed

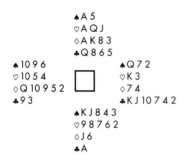

♠A 5
♡A Q J
◇A K 8 3
♣Q 8 6 5

♠10 9 6
♡10 5 4
◇Q 10 9 5 2
♣9 3

♠Q 7 2
♡K 3
◇7 4
♣K J 10 7 4 2

♠K J 8 4 3
♡9 8 7 6 2
◇J 6
♣A

a club back to the closed hand and repeated the heart finesse. This time MacLaren took his king and returned a low club allowing West to take the setting trick with the ♡10.

And what happens if East wins the first heart and returns a diamond, as good as anything? North wins and a high heart is played. When the ten doesn't drop, declarer has little option but to draw the last trump and continue with the ace and a spade to the jack hoping to find East with Q-x-x. As East had exactly that spade holding, the slam would have been made had MacLaren taken the first heart. Once again it was right to duck the first round of a repeatable finesse — even with a doubleton king! What courage.

Help me, partner

As Charles Goren mentioned many times in his numerous books, when you are playing with a weak partner, make your signals very clear. So when Billy Eisenberg gave me a discarding problem that I couldn't solve, I reminded him of what Goren had said.

Neither vul.

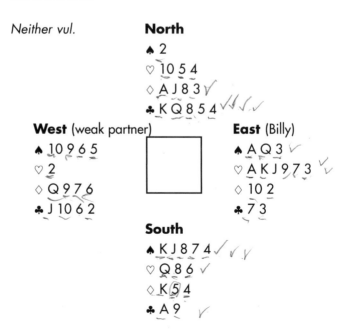

North
♠ 2
♡ 10 5 4
◇ A J 8 3
♣ K Q 8 5 4

West (weak partner)
♠ 10 9 6 5
♡ 2
◇ Q 9 7 6
♣ J 10 6 2

East (Billy)
♠ A Q 3
♡ A K J 9 7 3
◇ 10 2
♣ 7 3

South
♠ K J 8 7 4
♡ Q 8 6
◇ K 5 4
♣ A 9

West	North	East	South
		1♡	1♠
pass	2♣	2♡	2NT
all pass			

Opening lead: ♡2

Billy won the opening lead with the ♡K and played the ♡A. Timeout! I had to find a discard. Most players would simply discard a spade, but I was afraid that declarer might have AKQxx or AKJxx of spades in which case my discard would allow him to run the suit. On the other hand, if I threw a diamond and declarer had the king, I was giving up a trick in that suit. Finally, if I discard a club and declarer has the ace of that suit, I would never live that discard down either.

After much hemming and hawing (so if I did the wrong thing, at least Billy would know I was thinking about something), I made the worst possible discard, a club! Now, after winning the ♡Q, declarer was able to race off five club tricks and make the contract in a breeze.

Desperate to somehow find a way to pin my error on Billy, I told him if he had won the first heart with the ace and then played the king before playing a third heart I would realize that by his playing hearts in reverse order he was telling me that he had a spade entry so I could discard spades. When Billy saw how much help I needed on defense, he said he should have played the jack of hearts at Trick 1 and then I wouldn't have had to make any discards!

No, no, look over here...

Let's see how imaginative you are. Look at all four hands in the diagrammed deal below and try to figure out how South went down in 3NT. Note: South was an expert player and would not do anything crazy.

Neither vul.

North
- ♠ A Q 10 8 6
- ♡ 9 8
- ◇ Q J 8
- ♣ Q 4 2

West
- ♠ 7 3
- ♡ A J 6 5 3 2
- ◇ 6 3
- ♣ 10 7 3

East
- ♠ K J 5
- ♡ Q 4
- ◇ K 4 2
- ♣ J 9 8 6 5

South
- ♠ 9 4 2
- ♡ K 10 7
- ◇ A 10 9 7 5
- ♣ A K

West	North	East	South
			1◇
pass	1♠	pass	1NT
pass	2NT	pass	3NT
all pass			

Opening lead: ♡5

East played the queen of hearts and South won the king. Here is how South played the hand; you decide for yourself if he did anything wrong. South decided to live or die with the diamond finesse and not mess with the spades. Going for five tricks in spades, necessary if hearts aren't 4-4, requires West to have both spade honors.

Accordingly, South cashed the A-K of clubs at Tricks 2 and 3 and crossed to the ♠A to take the diamond finesse.

Kantar on Kontract

But a funny thing happened on the way to that diamond finesse, East dropped the king of spades under the ace!

Now who can blame South for thinking that it would be safer to play West for the ♠J than East for the ◇K? After all, if South can score five spade tricks, he doesn't need the diamond finesse. South crossed to the ◇A and ran the ♠9. Shock! East won the jack, returned a heart and six tricks later (the opponents were able to cash five more hearts and the ◇K, not to mention the ♠J), South wound up down three!

East had visualized declarer's problem and gave him a losing option. South took it — hook, line and sinker.

How loudly would you double if you knew your opponents were about to be set about 1100 points and you were playing for big bucks? If you are an ethical player, your double shouldn't shatter glass.

As good as it gets

Both vul.

North
♠ A K
♡ 2
◇ A Q 9 8 5 3
♣ A 7 4 2

West
♠ Q J 10
♡ A K Q 9 8
◇ 6
♣ K Q J 10

East
♠ 7 4 2
♡ 5
◇ K J 10 7 4
♣ 9 8 5 3

South
♠ 9 8 6 5 3
♡ J 10 7 6 4 3
◇ 2
♣ 6

```
           ♠ A K
           ♥ 2
           ♦ A Q 9 8 5 3
           ♣ A 7 4 2
♠ Q J 10              ♠ 7 4 2
♥ A K Q 9 8           ♥ 5
♦ 6                  ♦ K J 10 7 4
♣ K Q J 10           ♣ 9 8 5 3
           ♠ 9 8 6 5 3
           ♥ J 10 7 6 4 3
           ♦ 2
           ♣ 6
```

West	North	East	South
1♡	dbl	pass	1♠
2♣	2♢	pass	pass
dbl	pass	pass	2♡
dbl	all pass		

I was West. Can you possibly visualize my delight when this hand was actually passed out in 2♡ doubled, the opponents vulnerable no less? I tried to conceal a smile, but it was difficult...

Besides having the best trump holding in my life to make a penalty double, I was playing for thousands of dollars at the Riviera Masters Team of Four Championship in Las Vegas. We were in the semifinals near the end of a tight match and I was already spending my winnings (even if we came in second the prize money would be considerable).

I was even blessed with great leads in every suit. I finally decided on the ♣K and this is what happened. Declarer won the ace in dummy; ruffed a club; returned to a high spade; ruffed a club; crossed to the ♢A; cashed a second high spade; ruffed dummy's last club and then ruffed a spade in dummy.

Just in case you aren't counting, that makes eight tricks! I was left looking at my AKQ98 of hearts when the declarer graciously conceded the last five tricks. I was in shock. To further add to my misery, a kibitzer pointed out that if I had led a high heart and then shifted to any other suit, the hand would have been defeated one trick. Thanks a lot.